NIGHTSONGS FOR GAIA

Previous collections by James Byrne,
(excluding translations, collaborations
and edited books) include:

The Overmind, Broken Sleep Books, 2024
Of Breaking Glass, Broken Sleep Books, 2022
Places You Leave, Arc Publications, 2022
The Caprices, Arc Publications, 2019
Withdrawals, KFS, 2019
Everything Broken Up Dances, Tupelo Press, 2015
White Coins, Arc Publications, 2015
Soapboxes, KFS, 2014
Blood/Sugar, Arc Publications, 2009
The Vanishing House, Treci Trg, 2009
Passages of Time, Flipped Eye, 2003

James Byrne

Nightsongs for Gaia

New & Selected Poems

Arc Publications
2025

Published by Arc Publications,
Nanholme Mill, Shaw Wood Road
Todmorden OL14 6DA, UK
www.arcpublications.co.uk

978-1-911469-84-1 (pbk)

Design by Tony Ward

Cover painting:
'Nightsongs for Gaia' (acrylic, gouache & mixed media)
© James Byrne, 2025

Arc Publications UK & Ireland Series
Series Editor: Tony Ward

for my father,
Patrick T. Byrne
1948-2024

also for my daughter,
daydream & nightsong

CONTENTS

A NOTE ON THE SELECTION

I have attempted a somewhat stripped-down selection. What may constitute juvenilia is absent but for a poem from my first collection, published in my early twenties. Much of my subsequent writing has been supported by Arc Publications, therefore it feels fitting to publish a Selected Poems with them, completing a circle of time. I always wanted this kind of book to be published before I was fifty, I'm not sure why. Perhaps to clear the desk and keep moving. In my poetics, I've constantly been interested in the possibilities of change, moving through forms and aesthetic modes. I'd like to think *Nightsongs for Gaia* epitomises these kinds of shifts.

It was important to me to include texts not published on these shores before. During my writing life, I have sought various streams of publication. *White Coins* and *Everything Broken Up Dances* were published in the same year, in different countries with entirely different selections. The latter work has not been published in England until now, and it includes poems written out of poetry-related trips made to Myanmar, Libya and Syria. *Everything Broken Up Dances,* along with *The Overmind,* constitute the largest selection from single books here. In three poetry collections, I worked with materials such as photography and visual art. *The Caprices* is a 'dialogic ekphrasis' with Goya's 'Los Caprichos', *Places you Leave,* was published with original collages, and *Of Breaking Glass* includes photos from Death Valley, California. In this selection, I was keen to include images from all of these texts, since this is how they were first printed (albeit in colour). I have included the Goyas and one image apiece from *Places You Leave* and *Of Breaking Glass. Mythaca* and *Emanations* are bespoke, limited edition prints.

I acknowledge all the publishers and supporters of these works, full details of which are at the back of the book. I'd like to thank Tony Ward and Angela Jarman for all the work they have done, not merely their dedication to publishing my own poetry and translations, but how they have supported so many poets from across the world.

This book is dedicated to my father, who recently passed away, and my daughter Gaia, but it is also for Tony and Angela, and anyone else who has been kind enough to support my poetry. Meeting others along the way in my journey as a poet, in a communal and collaborative sense, finding solidarity and kinship, has been essential to the making of this book.

James Byrne, February 2025

from Passages of Time (2003)

THE TUNNEL SYNOPSIS

Life without music would be a mistake
F. Nietzsche

This is all I remember
There were mistakes and tunnels
And there were moments in-between
Where rhythm was a distant arc of gravity

After low-hushed cantillations of rain
The sun would suddenly flare up
Yet I would hear nothing
But silence on low volume

I don't know if the light was military
Or just a space that love couldn't occupy
I thought the Spanish castanets signified
The old boy cry of 'Wolf'

This is all I remember
Though no doubt there were other nights
Or other faces I avoided
As if they were agitated, or dog-boned

Backspacing, I think the darkness
Was something to be learned, like archery
Or loss, and I was the hypotenuse
Staring at absence, right-angled

Like an argument stitched to the womb.

from Blood / Sugar (2008)

APPRENTICE WORK

in memoriam, Peter Redgrove

The lithic who makes a pal in death
teaches me not to die so slowly.
'Many ways to become lineal' he says,
'to write The Sounding Book'.

Everything close as a finger thimble;
a lock of hair from Proserpine,
the tropics in Technicolor,
drumcliff tapped by a solitary cloud.

You lifted a finger over Gogol,
Little Russia droned bee-like.
And when they fired you up
Uhland took you in his colossal lung.

*

I've arrived late, apprentice imp,
to where you tripped out on yoga visions
and saw 22,000 years of art
insetted by a single flint;
to the Gale Chambers of the Vast Nose,
Cornish galleons tucked under the ocean like rain.

Who's to decide between glass economies
or the drowsy pulp of the sea?
It ties the forensic squad in knots –
the way groundswell fattens
from a single rock, remakes itself
into delicate gemstone.

*

These days *The Book of Thresholds*
fits firm for a pillow,
it wakes me with an empire's relish.

No identity preference, no thumb guide.
Only scent variations,
each murmurous, each perennial.

The footnotes appear Pythagorean
cupid seminaries / vanity carnivals
vs. GIGANTIC LABOUR.

No monument decision –
nothing on the slumberous reek
of a salmon polished by the sun.

*

We apprentice poets need an innovator,
'verbal haemoglobin', not a casket key.
I repeat the only rule you knew as mantra:

everything is invitation.

RECOVERY

Let me imagine you coming home
from the dark, between body and mind,

making evidence of yourself
the way a tree waves up from its shadow.

There are dinner-halls you have silenced
with a single spark of wit,

there are men you have governed
through pure scent, pure posture.

Now for your most difficult trick:
to restart a life that ends by turning into gold.

In September (the month that tends to all others)
let me be able to conjure your best side,

to have some kind of grip on the intactness
of living, the way mirrors do.

AIR TERMINALS

for Sandeep

...I dreamed
of a page in a book containing the word bird and I
entered bird.

ANNE CARSON, 'Gnosticism I'

Reading how Mansfield claims the word *air*
is to live in it.

Pure scheme vs. science anxiety.

Not the *duck of a boy* emphatic
nor the rich-leaning Rosemary,

more a chance to inhabit
adrenal pressure –
six hours of braided sky
pushed through cloud braille.

*

How to steady up when all at once
air batches you out to crash phobias,

night after night,
wing tensions grazing your head?

*

Small curve of trust in a child's joy at architecture.

At the terrorist check
threshold and counter-threshold –

a sparrow's fear of total sunlight,
a studious approach to Boeing assemblies.

*

Carefully your ration array of clothes
checked in tight folds   touches

and is how air means,

clipped around the roots of a hand

as you look back gesturing
once   twice   finally.

*

Air as the steadying of addiction:
how to breathe as the shadow dips?

Air-guides to breakers at the logic gate
the perfect crime, always getting away.

Evidences in landing vapour –
the movement of my hand on your back that says

'go'.

*

The route I take I take on foot,
afraid and tenderly loyal.

At the ventilation tunnel
the smooth saturation of air vocals,
every tenor, decorous.

Your flaunting of altitude
is strictly west-hugging.

How the difference tells?

There was a cold bitter taste in the air
and the new-lighted lamps looked sad.

DAYS OF 1973

The chambers of his heart filling with faces.
Mine. Yours. A stranger trails around a corner.
Fuming echoes circle a pair who argue
In some fiery tongue… A conversation
I broke off some years ago drifts up.
J. D. McClatchy

Fear was my father, Father Fear
Theodore Roethke

I'll tell you, but not here.

*

To walk in tall shadows of the forest
is to invite further shadows.

The light astonishes from every exit-point.

*

Where the garden adjoins the house
by the crooked trunk of a Box Elder –
a father's priestly assurance…

If I've learnt anything since your mother…
man's lot is the muddied field, or no field.

*

Through the Elder's pinnate a crash of sun
parleys your temples –

the samara wings sigh,
a dense calculated sigh.

*

For twenty years the abysm expanded, hard time
snared a decade....

'The kettle yearns for the mountain / The soap for the sea'

*

Your eyes are solemnised,
a colder blue.

On history they come and go.

But the mind – cunning enough to *act* on love –
audits and impels history,
mosses every stone.

*

I left the house with my own stare daggering your spine.

(...My brother and I hid knives under our shorts in the court
lobby.

We were trained for the script.

To get off wrist-slapped was 'No Access'.)

*

In his shed study,
a simple swinging wire turns to metronome...

...What happened during the Christmas of 1973...?

...There's a picture of my mother – cross-legged, all bones,
shrunken to her wits.

*

(...) *We was less than your age* (...) *Hard to relive now* (...)

(…) *She could temper the Saints, y'know*

*

A decided jury-master,
the allegations stood –

Children for alcohol.
A cruiserweight finesse….

We rolled down the stairs – she and I –
three weeks from birth.

What if I was born then and what for
in our vanishing house?

*

This *is* access –
we are a mismatched couple tethered by blood.

*

His head is peppery and veined like marble,
something solid to look at,
yet doubling up as breakable.

*

If I break now
I am locked in for life.

*

(The notebook is fluent as the tongue.

I keep a photograph of my grandmother
on which reads a quote from Lowell's *History*
You were [his] *airhole.* '73.)

*

To equate such instances with all men fetches strength:

When men happen together
there's always some kind of tremoring business.

*

Cheap getaway, he fumbles with the door –
a side-glimpsed grin icteric with victory.

*

If it cannot be translated as what it was…
a 'version' empowers me:

Pain is inevitable…
(how we clown after it)

Suffering is optional
(the first rule of confession).

*

In attic rooms of my father's house
I am everywhere and shushed quiet.

The smiles on the faces of blanched photographs
are proud and importedly Irish.

*

My grandmother's face
resumes in my face and
feeds the ghost between us.

*

There's more where that came from…

I tore the cheque to shreds,
scattered it on your lawn.
It flew through the air
and held like confetti.

*

What it is…

…like a kind of falling…

I have failed you with my life.

SESTINA FOR R

Dawn and again your voice cracks
like a vessel too thin for certain
vibrations. Demisting the window,
you rock gently from side-to-side,
your hand waving with a rhythm
that holds you to it as if by a drug.

Your doctor prescribes the same drug
on every visit, widening the cracks
in your downcast face. Deadly rhythm.
If treatment and health go side-by-side,
untreatable is your face at the window.
You're the same sunk vessel, for certain.

Like a vessel too thin for certain
vibrations, you re-alight in '91: a drug
binge at The Brain. Memory's window
props open, reconfiguring wisecracks
from the promo video. On the outside
you were a zeitgeister, the rhythm

of the club – the core of its rhythm.
What plans you had. Fame, for certain.
But the pilled-up crew at your side
guided a thin vessel. Love was the drug
fooled by its addiction. The cracks
widen in your profile at the window.

Who are you waiting for at the window?
The streetlamps click off to the rhythm
of a lit horizon. Chimney cracks
proffer terraced light to a certain
vibration, until the light, like a drug,
fires the body, flush full on the side

of your face (as if warmed from inside).
This is your life at the window.
Fear-hogged, shocked quiet by drug
after drug. Frail now, less of rhythm,
like a vessel too thin for certain
vibrations. Furrowed are the cracks.

Outside, traffic cargoes to a rhythm.
You hear a ghost sonata tap the window.
I listen in closely until your voice cracks.

A PRIVATE GARDEN

Early to rise for knowledge of the garden – for the fringe of a gossamer hammocking. I watched the painful sum of its catch and knew the eeriness of death for the first time. The spider trapezed his web, a thin ball of coal discovering its prey in filigrees of ash. His victim, trapped in the jewel case, huddled appallingly for its life. A sudden drop in the breeze and the kill was fished clean. Books have never taught me these things.

*

Seated between the knuckled limbs of the tree house, I spied on a swarm of wasps nuzzling at apples; their glassy colour-code and spoiling tails cranked with venom – emblematic fire. In France, later that year, my mother broomed a nest and was fanged by an army of them. A quickly pumped prescription pulled her back from an inch of life. Full of the feast, a wasp landed on my hand and looked at me like a god, perfectly evil.

*

For what seemed an era, I clutched at the giant slab to win one look under its shadow. With a gravelly belch the stone pulled loose and revealed to me its secret archive – the dark unendingness of a disused well. Peering in, I conjured the anaemical fix of my father's stare and shouted down until my face burnt red: *This is my garden!* There was music then. The chambered echoes passed through me to their reunions.

from White Coins (2015)

HISTORIA

moving on or going back to where you came from
Amy Clampitt

it is not the substance of a man's fault
it is the shape of it
is what lives with him, is what shows
Charles Olson

a room crammed   with sharp toys

a field zesty with fire

history as historia

cool as a shot to the mouth

*

in pinched shoes
cataleptic

merely to show up

the birdlime viscidity of the garden
the scalpel-like finger
of a shrivelled leaf –

not accusatory
shadowed only
by itself
not pointing
towards a balance-act
but balancing

*

I was six and made of violins
stumped
by metronomic light

I wanted to energise him away
like glucose
globed
into whiteness –

a voice spoken slantwise
but faraway –

sleeping it off

I travelled in the dark
so as not to be seen

*

dusk-nervousness
in what is unclaimed

I wait and fail
paying off warders
at your door –

the thrillbox
of birthdays

whalecalls from waterclotted
condensation

the gazebladed kitchen

the uplander silences of television

blackish fingernails
from window mould

eyes goggled
towards a lit hearth
fringe fraying

or cupping at the curtain frame
fearful of fire
on the domestic zodiac

*

how the air divides
like cutting a loaf –

as much childed
as fevered

left alone
in the dry season

to feed from the day's nutrients –

naphtha mirage
over the wheatfield
at sunset

foxfur grinning on a spidersweb

dialysis of rain
inside a garden well

equal to breath

*

– to hear the substance of the earth
to know its shape

blessèd as an egg
and yet –

and yet bombarded
by the radio impulse
of survival

the whistlework of money –

her ivied hair
trenched at the oven or
admonished at the fire-grate

*

shuffle-worn cards
blanked-out letters
from the on-dead

how life tickles the palm
at twenty

dreaming up worser devils

thinking the lesser disease might be
loneliness –

no-one to ignite
the red-eyed bird
of your mind

no-one told you why
love
blunts

*

if the bones sing

if chaos is chaos
returned –

no atom nuclei
no definitive cure

*

enter fortune

a ransacked house
half-emptied –

that which remains
preserved in boxes

now bulges
like a museum

*

baffled voices   vow trounces
– as if from any archive –

I lean over and touch my ear
to the grid complex –

like hearing ritual cannibalism
in the byways of a river

from **ECONOMIES OF THE LIVING**

The Hummingbird

Hazelnut. Feathered black, brownish and
green. Traitor to the flower press, luxuriant
but uselessly sportive, uselessly fluttering.

Female's the architect. Male: a panicked
fetcher of cottoned twigs, vegetable fibres.
Skivvy for cloudhouses suspended in air.

A family of silken music caged by Labat
for rats. We are purposed for pleasure.
Touch the wings to kill its instrument.

The Horse

Europe's incommode: it is not free
to roam continents like the horse did.
Tack, yield, never knowing winter.

Turnstiled like prisoners of the sedan.
Tractable and familiar. The Bedouin
shares his tent with foals, surrenders

his courser mare to the French consul.
The things a horse has traded for gold.
Closely farried, shockpools for eyes.

The Orangutan

Brute like us. Brute of the woods.
Sternly countenanced then maligned
like cracked hutches of the counselled.

Epitaphic, ritualized buriers and so
larger than most men. Upwards of you
unfolding a napkin and as Buffon said:

fond of comfits but, unlike the baboon,
clever to show a man where the door is.
Trained servants, able to work as we do.

Mortality

What makes for strong pillars? Roots
like crooked fangs and the spectacle
of letting blood. Those Nietzchean debts

collected, as if to pay what you owe
were pure as the horizoned backdrop
to some Parthenonic theatre. Death

is in the world, stand up, weep together
or longer. Insects sport all day in the sun.
Easterly winds nip the verdure nightlong.

Heaven

Life is good and there's plenty of it.
Hymnals of rose and thorn. Henbane
doesn't bloodspeckle the white lilacs.

Barbauld saw heaven with cherubim
flying on fired wings. Borges craved
endless library shelves. Hold on hope.

Son of Jesse, shepherd king, with what
language do we say goodbye to ourselves?
What bell sings another hour of her?

from **RIMBAUD VILLANELLES**

14 Rue Nicolet

What is wrong with the ex-pats and the French?
Only two of us show up for The Rimbaud Walk
despite the ballyhoo: *A 5 Mile Drift on Absinthe.*

Sure, there's a grin in the wind, but what prudence
nowadays; no surprise the UMP still shun a plaque
for 14 Rue Nicolet. What is wrong with the French?

Rimbaud, at sixteen, arrived here from the Ardennes
for havoc in the house of Verlaine's new stepparents,
and for Verlaine himself, who was gone on absinthe.

At night, they stumbled home under the low-lit lamps
surveyed by Verlaine's jilted *chanson,* Mathilde Mauté,
who despised the bad manners of these mountain French.

It is a house too prim for bohemians or boy peasants
agreed the inlaws. Lice-ridden, Rimbaud slept on the lawn
naked in the sun, peeled to his ribs, popeyed on absinthe.

Mathilde saw her life slide away whilst pregnant.
Verlaine threw little Georges at the wall and walked.
This house is a shamed house, censored by the French.
Before Rimbaud, Verlaine was hooked on absinthe.

8 Royal College Street

Lot of the 'infernal bridegroom', of the red herring,
sold by a blind veterinary, then torn and desecrated
by Ogun and his vandal workmen. Attic of Verlaine

vs Rimbaud, where landlady Smith heard screaming
from 'Parisian gentlemen', their knife-tips slashed,
towel-wrapped, until the final slap of a wet herring.

The site endures because of months of campaigning:
McDevitt and Dun on the BBC, in Paris and *Le Monde*
assembling the French Embassy and, pro-Verlaine,

daring the council to revamp no. 8 as a publishing
house, with a floor where 'love must be re-invented'
and an absinthe bar. On the doorstep, grilled herring,

citations of 'Vagabonds', the formula still missing,
an ear pricked for the resale, hearing it landlorded
to Corby, a Camden Tory, who derided Verlaine,

if not Rimbaud, and would 'conserve' by subletting
no. 8, amiable still to a resident poet, so he pretended.
Capitalistically, Corby stuffed our ideas in a red herring.
For £1600-a-week, cut-price: Rimbaud and Verlaine.

INSIDE THE HOUSE OF LU SAN

Inside the house of Lu San on Minn Street
a cat's paw swipes at a fishbowl and breaks
the trellis web between two toothbrushes –
nothing in the world is as mean as death.

Which does not mean the mildew-matted
base of a white metal bed, its edges stilted,
stretched beneath a bust of Christ / Socrates.

Twinned fragility: how the sculpture looms
above books dimmed in mahogany light,
from where she peek-a-boos, stage right –
concertina of a daughter, her little lobes

of feet stirring the kitchen's citrusy air.
A transbotanical face, shyly in soft focus –
life to the mythomania of life's possessions.

from Everything Broken Up Dances (2015)

1977

Star Wars premiered as they cut the exiguous flap of my umbilical.

THE KING IS DEAD ran *The Herald* and the midwife handed over the genesis
of my unfledged, unwhimpering body.

In the carrycot of my mother's arms, hissing privately with birth,
I cried nothing, confessed nothing.

It was the year of the snake and *The Spy Who Loved Me* –
the year Zulfiqar Bhutto was ousted by the Bond villain ul-Haq.
The year Steve Biko was clubbed to death in custody.

Fidgety among the hangings, my grandfather peered down longingly
for 90 minutes at the pitch below the hospital where Rangers were leading
Wanderers.

A Rangerette herself, when I was born my mother asked the Doctor for the score –
'It's a classic match: eight fingers, two thumbs.'

75,000 fans lined the streets of Memphis for the King's funeral.
500 million tuned into their small screens
as the Queen's Jubilee carriage trundled up The Mall.

My father was late to the maternity ward.
He arrived bearing a thin deck of lilies, whitely inflamed from their sprigs.

It was the year President Carter pardoned draft dodgers and George Willig
(a.k.a. 'The Human Fly') climbed the World Trade Center.

I was speechless and ready to alight, preserved by a flambeau of luck.

This was the year Sadat became the first Arab leader to visit Israel seeking a
peace deal –

the year my brother, on hearing the altarpiece of our house break in its glass,
shelved us together, under the bed.

'When will it ever stop?' I heard one voice whisper to another.
My mother scooped up my egesting mess from the floor.

The year ended in a clappering of bells.

Amnesty won the Peace Prize.
The Cold War was inscrutable.
On and on it went.

ONE / ANOTHER

One sighs heavily down the telephone
Another pours the assassin's quicksand

One leaves the garrison lonely as a bullet
Another fills white tubs with kerosene

One is surveyed from the border glass
Another guards against the darkness of trees

One clinks to the enemy's thimble
Another fantasizes death in a flyway

One slugs the sitter at his pianoforte
Another takes shade under a fig tree

One discerns bloodiness from the siren
Another brandishes the manacles

One juggles dust between his hands
Another combusts the basecamp

WILD DESERT THYME

for Sandeep

For your sprigs of wild desert thyme
we convoy to the sea-gardened city of Sabratha
earth-deepness of pillared centuries
ghostwalking Greco-Roman walls
kitchen-quarters
dungeons
the trembling concave of its amphitheatre
gold as dusk
re-casting the invisible chorus
and backdropping away
to the distant Maghreb
the cooled winter gulf
where I dip my feet
amid the rockscrub

then afterwards
led through the cream museum
where my face sang
in the glasshouse of the tragic actor
and was neither healed nor lured
by the attending lyre of Bacchus
or Concordia's matted scarf of serpents
I sat in the mosaic hall of the three graces
smelling out the tarry bitterness of human meat

*

A daydream woken off by gunfire
(another deferred wedding?)
hurried to the bus
in a cloudrack of dust
to relative calm
the stricken village of Surman
brown limbs of shelled apartments
still wearing the massacre effect
our creaturely sicknesses
old as Jupiter's beard trestles

exact middle of the sun-burnished street
a hunched woman
improvised to thinness
harried sacks of grain
our driver honked her to a fright
and she spilled half the carryweight
then turned to level back at us
staring from under a black shawl
open and enormous in her silence

*

For your wild desert thyme
we took the checkpoint road
beneath the Nafusa mountain
(an old Romanic route
straight as tightened rope)
on one side burst a hundred-yard of camels
triumphantly riderless
and from the smeary west window
all the way to the checkpoint
a scrapyard of tanks
ditched in the roadside's gullet
their armaments plundered
overturned
khaki bleeding bulletholes
and scorched 4x4s
piled five high
potent as ash in the dustpath
in the chancelleries
of war and hunger

*

The checkpoint soldiers
of the FREE LIBYA ARMY
drew Kalashnikov's
nervous in a kind of antique fear
circling the vehicle at first
until we paid them off

with victory signs
and Ashur's laugh of the honeybee

on the lassoing road of the mountain
WELCOME TO YEFREN
graffiti'd in English
Berber and Arabic
THANK GOD FOR EVERYONE'S SAFETY...
PUT UP YOUR HEAD... YOU ARE FREE LIBYA
trucks on stilts
cracked gas-pipes
and grey-sprayed wheelbarrows
outside the hardware shop
where the shopkeeper taps his pen
on the window grill
and a boy fills a barrow with dead mortar shells

*

For your wild desert thyme
the Algazeer re-hoist their flag
(rainbow of yellow blue red and green)
the Algazeer who have farmed this mountain
for eight hundred years
and who survived the war
by living in ancient caves
beneath the stonebase of their ancient city
Gaddafi banned the Algazeer
burnt their flag
cut the water and food supply
says Sālim
spiderishly nimble on the tumbled rocks
pointing to a road
that does not meet and has not met
for eight hundred years

and it is from this road
for your wild desert thyme
that I kneel down
past the abandoned bootlegger path

where the olive trees sing
from the desert's hymnbook
and the caves hold the scent
of a just-skinned carcass
and the synagogue rises
from a camouflage of sand

*

The taste of the future
is history
tethered inside a green box
a volcano of perfume
wind-sculpted
embalmed with leaves
like a tree…
open it

MALLAJAH

Mute for minutes – keeffak – ana bikhayr – note guttural Rs – gobbets on Hikmet – genius or personality – the butterfly insignias of Darwish – not a *Burden* – non-verbal – bricabrac Arabic – can be a blessing – sometimes – scan the table for unpayable translators – sh'kran habibi – cannot learn a language just by hearing it – Spanish maybe – sh'kran – wide glossy smile – all I can say – sh'kran habibi – drinking mate through a scolding straw – gets rid of Arak – gets in teeth – tamam – medicine *and* breakfast – need water – you stir it like this – clockwise is anticlockwise – like the alphabet – see – sh'kran – what better life than the life in *this* valley – whiff of Mediterranean over the olive grove – where are you from Hamad – hypnotism in gasblue eyes – what he said makes perfect sense but cannot be translated into English – time suspended by a conjurer's trick – literally then – the children of my first painting never forget to smile – my teeth are cleaner here – my teeth rot every day in Lebanon – skin like the valley's rockface – remember where you stand – the men of three villages built this festival – stone by stone – some died carrying the rocks – could be the seventh century – over one thousand will fill this valley tomorrow night – half or more from three villages – there – there – there – we've moved on but the point is still to be made – nothing rots on its own says Hamad – poor translation – do you like Tartous – can attract waitresses but not yet order any food – what about Damascus – walked up Qasioun in strawburning heat – didn't Cain slay Abel up there – holiest balcony I ever stood from – Telemnin on one side – the Old City islanded in the distance – gold and whitelight – pleated gold – can't tell you that now can I – what about the barbwire road with the green tower roadblocked by soldiers – off the map – don't wait to eat – eat – sh'kran – pita is the life of the table – I offer the basket to a gaptoothed boy – calls me Sahibi – a face of one pure note – wears half the paint lost from the canvas – twill of reds pinks oranges grays – *An Olive Tree Lit by Thorns* – sh'kran – habibi – tamam – preface / footnote / trio – everything said in a museum of accents – haven't read Mafouz – haven't listened to Fairuz driving through the dark valley at night – outsider – out-majoritied – but we are all family here – all same – octopi of embraces – cigarette – sh'kran – Amira hides spirit tears – divorce pending – man has to give consent – three years – *three years* – you would do fine if you didn't have a girlfriend – red appled cheeks – Firas circles the room with a mothy dance – at the far end someone is singing – clefts of banned Syrian folk – Sammi's mother transforms into a veritable Venus when she sings – how to pronounce that – *Yaall daar* – spits like a soothsayer over her tahini bowl – her name means longest night of the year – you see how it is – sh'kran – President Assad like a king with a million eyes – a million ears – translation: please habibi – not the poem about Iraq

VARIATIONS ON DARKNESS

How slowly dark comes down on what we do.
THEODORE ROETHKE, 'In Evening Air'

1.

If you drink from the shuck of the storm
you will always be tainted by its darkness.

2.

The lacquered surface of the canal at night
is darker than the darkest shroud of Jesus.

3.

One thing darker than the roses' shadow
– the cold fire of the roses after thunder.

4.

Far murkier than possession – the shiphold
shackled to the hells of human darkness.

5.

The panmongolist was so afraid of the dark
he asked to be buried in a candlelit coffin.

6.

The stare he gave his wife whilst dinnering
was like a bullet shot through with darkness.

7.

When the rusted machete cut back the cane
it sharpened darkly in the emperor's silence.

8.

Amnesially waiting in the cinema's darkness
– it cannot be separated out from loneliness.

9.

A death-pecked cry darkens the entire city
and is hoisted through the shrieking world.

from EPITAPHS FOR A NEW CENTURY

1.

on the count of GO run for your life.
apply elevated heels for a better view
and remember no-one tips the gallows.
in television county ancient stones
weigh us down. the axe cools beside
new recipes for double-butter muffins.
rise from the armchair to hear agony
creak. nothing exists beyond the bridge
of your nose. minutes refined by sand.
anchoresses in limousines. old trades.
flesh money. from spiders under glass
to backbone tumours – shared breath –
enough for a pulse in the rough houses.
behind thick red smoke the informants
appear proud as parents at a home plate –
each wears a silver watch on his left hand.

4.

milk drains off and friendships creak
with the past like an old bullock cart.
the dream of the cobbler possesses me.
Duchamp in Acheron or Dostoyevsky
in London – we want to live in the sea
that is not our home. no patron saints
only laser-eyed community directors.
the kids are turning into chrysalides.
work – *wrekan* – meant to persecute.
its variant *wreaked.* robots of *rabota*
love not sleep lest you come to poverty.
the man our village calls Polish Mick
trembles curtains and twitches the whip.
it's action that makes a community.
the good shoe will fit like a readymade.
what cannot be sold to us is fog-logic.

5.

aquariums dance well not the fish.
winter early this year and so much
bad weather as if it were between us.
why is it some painters suffer more
when painting breezes while others
can hear seeds clicking in a field.
Van Gogh's sunned orchard beside
tile cats laving in late afternoons.
Shostakovich suckerpunched by the 14th
same as for Nietzsche patting stirrups.
activist or terrorist but do not blemish
the human canvas. be still and spectral
as woodsmoke or grubby as old jokes.
like the one where Guy Fawkes laughs
at his own funeral – the most honest man
who would ever set foot in parliament.

6.

girl among the hawthorns wait for me.
the bluebells are speaking in Spanish.
let's clear the table for a game of cards.
forgetfulness devours. thunder is luck.
there's always more kindling to burn –
stave off the heat by closing shutters.
practice the disclosure of photographs.
in the bright fields we have shat upon
in the boiled-down effigies of nature
open-air aviaries. blood on hessian.
what does it mean to return to a native
place. pennants of memory. a river.
family trees still logjam the Goree
caste fishermen steady up spears.
so much for the redemption of Libra
rising. the hidden filigrees of gold.

THE OPPONENT

Though it is a scarlet day my opponent wears his topcoat in the park. Old squirmy enthusiast, always nodding out of sight from the pack; today he is an onlooker in redwood shade. With a cool, apprehending finger, he points up to the springy torso of a beech tree. I study its green hydra-headedness and there, among the forked branches, an American Redstart, nested, and so it appears, unable to fly from its black and orange overalls. *Share our impediments,* asks the opponent in his broad, larval accent and wide, footsore smile. *Tell me,* I retort, *which of you lives greater today: autocrat or lizard.* A long Arian cackle before he readopts the face of an Aquarian. Does evil cluster inside evil. Was he born with a wick for trapdoors. I sneaker to a foothold, cup the Redstart, and with a quick movement of my wrist snap down on its neck. For a moment, so brief, too brief, something bordering desire remains inside the bird until the final flick-flack release of its fantail. *Beautiful* says the opponent, with a calm, iniquitous stare. *Almost exactly as if I would have done it.*

from **EVERYTHING BROKEN UP DANCES**

1.

And what of the insatiable sadness of stepfathers

And her smeary mascara that slicks the rain

And the daub of red tape infecting a clean health bill

And what's with these singe-effects from the capitol bomb

And the dead telephone at the ear of a new generation

And when his welcoming smile widened like a crossbow

And how a wise oak lets in the new moon's eye

And the motel room with a stubbly kiss

And the jailbird in the yard firing rubber bullets

And the rotting fence surrounding the national comedy

And a white rosette for the bawdy little rich girl

And to wake after a decade shouting 'malady malady!'

And the weekday orgasm of the academic coming on a Sunday

And how the crucifiers were struck by womb lightning

And if the volcano would chirr just a little

And as they played jacks in the matron's office

And but for the sewage a smell of sweet sycamore

And the mind's polka played all through November

And the love gone to pot now cooks up the lobster

And with the years already shortening as it is

4.

Yes the niblets surpass the dinner party anecdotes

Yes a little more bling might clinch the swing states

Yes the icicle-eyes of the ad-man are to warm you

Yes another day in the life of Adam and his pet snake

Yes the unopened page cannot be properly read

Yes a concrete staircase that can withstand a full-speed jet plane

Yes the hologram at the desk is your attentive web check-in

Yes the Ministry of Circuses is the Ministry of Culture

Yes Genghis Khan is buried here there and everywhere

Yes even the foulest water puts out the fiercest fire

Yes Hitler stroked his dog 'Wolf' in the bunker

Yes the art auctioneer is a punch-clock for the business tycoon

Yes a cargo-load of diplomacy to buy up the munitions site

Yes the church chandeliers can be seen as heavenly merchandise

Yes the librarian did it with the vicar in the green room

Yes just keep nodding along to the coffeepot bohemians

Yes we are living in the era of squeaky arses

Yes the tattoo above her buttocks reads DOGGY

Yes Artistic Impact woos the faculty committee

Yes nobody's perfect and he was just another nobody

5.

But for all the snowballs thrown in hell

But for every human grain in the Ganges

But the devil could give singing lessons to a voice like that

But the icecap reduced to a yellowy plume

But the louder they shout the less quietly we will come

But why do the dum-dums keep getting ahead

But they say dollars are better than real change

But what if the fifth commandment means Don't Trust Your Children

But brother fire says death is hereditary

But what if there was a law on hunger

But because the hardest thing in the world is to walk straight

But these summer rumba kids don't want to talk about it

But in Sanskrit the Empire ruled very differently

But why more admiral statues when the roads are so shoddy

But the electoral headwind is for fresh cuts

But the plucked eye on the end of a cocktail stick

But to know more intimately the murderer's brute joy

But the ewe licks the feet of the lion (its natural enemy)

But the gardener knows why the bud's heart is bloody

from Withdrawals (2019)

2

What grows inside of you
festers inside of me. I live
like something missing
in the conventional reading
of a book, irreparably repaired
for the latest knuckle ride.
Torpor lethargy at the public
feast. Stench of a war duke.
Skunk effluvial and aflare
with carnal optimism, I want
to take a bath in your body.
To be washed clean.

4

Head rush. Shudder rush.

You say that modern life is *always* busy
                                        all of the time.

          So busy this.

Disturbance of sea-swill. Beached kelp, strung up and knotted –

the negotiating table spread out like evolutionary error.

You echo duty   friendship as opposition.

But I am your baby. I am your gingled yolk.

12

Silence, say something. Tell me a story without touching the floor.

When your packages arrive we cannot open them. We hold them with the blindness of our fingers, smell for soil.

So much to tell you, I cannot tell you. They refuse to touch one another in this liminal city.

I breathe anonymously, quiet as a backcloth. I see you spread out in the peacock coat of an evening, sleep fading to black.

Call me in the morning, not the evening. Your voice, within walking distance, walks away.

24

Left brain   a family of skin.
Right brain   severance intersected.

We meet for a while. Do not meet.
I peel from the blue light of your body

into this black square of thinking,
where what is held holds nothing.

Between sea and seafoam,
between sleep and sleepwalking,

I move, on the edge of Europe,
Towards nobody, towards you.

from The Caprices (2019)

Nobody knows himself

Wear a face to look more like yourself.
Clothes, flesh and voice are all false.
I am the mystery, occasioned as myself,
compound volatile, sewn at the mouth.
Look me in the eye and I am elsewhere,
I sleep, silent as ink. Ancestral breath
blows clean the curtain. Dreams are
embroidered from people that exist.

The sleep of reason produces monsters

Now that the state legitimises hate,
a wakeful trump of doom thunders
valley deep (where are the Blake's
and Miltons now?). Crisis of mirrors
where my neighbour reasons only
with himself: a hissing face, chained
to sleep in a star's coda. A fantasy,
that whatever is pure is ENGLAND.

Hobgoblins

Another kind of people hobgoblins
the minds of little men. No Bunyan
fiend is he who frightens a maiden
of ancient privilege. Happy as no-one
but a freak. Hand of Puck who jokes
sweetly unfree to sweeten a Dukedom.
The wrong face in the oldest village
is another's. A goblin is no Athenian.

Swallow it, dog

Name? Interrogation's blackest sun.
Age? Old as vexation. Address? Fire
ash of moon. Hot schist of mountain.
Why are you here? Vertigo as desire.
Excess of loneliness. Death's syringe.
What do you see when you look at us?
Bone-light behind the eyes. Swinge
of terror's lance. A man on his knees.

Look how solemn they are!

Choose not I or you but she with him. Hollywood likes it under a barcode sky best of all [insert possessive pronoun here]. Raptorial cackle. The predatory cocksnook squats on her back. The sun says nothing, sinking into a white cloud made of bone. Her tells her, tell no-one. If you are my friend, I am your friend.

It is time

With a grimace then, to go without
inhaling the sun. But I served my time,
I swallowed the jailors key in my mouth.
Now the fire sign rises, it's only old men
who shriek in the flames. I'm not like them.
When I close my eyes they open on you,
bright in the Puerta del Sol. Bell chimes.
Ten in the morning. Silencio. Silencio…

from Places You Leave (2022)

COX'S BAZAR

You plant the jackfruit's anonymous, nubbled face and wait in the boiling sand for something to happen.

A goat's eye flashes gold. A girl swings on the tubewell for a cup of water.

You plant peas to grow in the monsoon and put on your best shirt. Yellow for optimism.

What is missing about the blank page is denied. Decimated, you would like to cohere.

Inside an airless, windowless hut, you try to re-write Stevens: Ten Ways of Looking at a Passport. 'I have never seen a passport, how does it begin?'

Toothmarks in the linebreak. You want to put the art back into heart.

When your brother ran towards the Tatmadaw, crying 'Jayzu, Jayzu', you turned and ran. Jahaj of air. Jail, lock and key.

Without 'art', it's just 'he', meaning brother. Come here, brother, but he isn't listening.

Your mother bribes the army guard to write a letter, asks about the non-trial. Will the guard deliver? Hope's lottery. There is no policy on answering the letters or the law. The page a windbreak. To write is to petition.

The 'I' severs you in the photograph, so we repose. Someone else must always be next to you. You cannot work alone.

Cyclonic clangour of rain. Sword-water in the Naf. The helicopter pumps into Bangladeshi airspace and fires on anyone swimming away.

The poem bare as a pulse, a knife. Siblings in graves.

The poem bare as a knife, a pulse.

Your father remains stuck on the border. 'Genocide Zone'. Nobody is reporting from there, so nothing is said.

The child draws pictures of a burning house. Singing out of history in makeshift schools.

You plant and write. Plant and write. What else is there to do? Peas on your roof grow beside the ashfire. You knot back the twine and forecast clouds.

You write: 'blot out', 'jail of air' and the words mean the same in the morning. Myanmar waits for the incendiary. The Saudis send money for guns. When you 'like' the post about ARSA, your cousin gets a note under his hut.

'Ze zaga añra félai ay zaígoí'. 'There are places we leave' you say. 'There are places we never leave. Home is a dream inside a nightmare'.

The first line of your first poem begins: 'I am afraid of someone I don't know'.

Last night your mother peeled back the tarpaulin and asked: 'what are you doing, my son, why can you not sleep? Sleep!' And you replied: 'Emily Dickinson, Emily Dickinson'.

You ignore the honking of the UNHCR truck, check the download speed for '100 Poets in English' (to learn poetry, to learn English). Reload.

Already they are looking to blame the same someone. The Chinese highway needs to be paid.

Looking at you. Between Paan branches brittled by soil erosion.

Why is it you live in the middle of the largest refugee camp in the world and they're calling it 'a lost treasure', a 'forgotten' national park?

They ask you to plant trees to 'save the environment'. Yes, you think. A few more trees to hide the smell of the latrine.

How do you write about 'environment'? You try for the present, the sensory, but your eyes sting, your ears hum and the smell is flesh and smoke.

'I want to write about family, but I have no family.'

The idea of the eternal traveller does not hold. To think of poetry as orphic. To unthink memory: to unriver the severed head.

As if the world were a wound flapping its bandages.

As if the world were a wound. As if…

You wake up and poke your pen through the ash.

English ale. 'Dada eta ki gari?' High speed trains. This is where I am going.

An envelope stuffed with Taka. A bookmark. To hold nothing, to hold your place in the book.

from **ISTANBUL → GAZIANTEP**

for F

Guilty as privilege. To be here where you should be. But not here. Weighing kofte bari, cemen otu behind the splint-fillings of Yeni mosque. No words for no word from the smuggler broker. To call. Not to call. To be left waiting on the end of the line. To uselessly pull apart Kurdish rugs, haggling over prices as they price you up. Money rots. Your elders are cashed out / into the unravelling bribe. Call it what it is. Wary over Whatsapp [Delete this.........Delete]. Red blush tomatoes slip too easily down the throat. Mesopotamian host eyes the cost of an oil truck stuttering across the Bosporus. You are crammed around your uncle's tv watching Premier League re-runs. Choose wisely not to celebrate, sliding in the winning goal on Cox's beach. You turn your face into someone else. Your name into Bangla. Send the visa a week ahead but still the flight grounds another and again. On Büyükada, a Turkish flag severs the landing boat. You wait, linger at water like the Marmaran sea tunnelling into white haze. To hear no news changes nothing. Everything. A crow shatters the window pane. Stares at its own reflection. Unable to fly.

Dilek Taşi. Place a hand on the wish column. The sweating column. Laugh out your tears on the weeping column. Scree your hand anti-clockwise. Cool it on a marble jar from Pergamon. If the muezzin's voice holds until the last note, it rings for truth. But whose? One wish. To walk freely through Imaret's gate. As if leaving were simplicity. One footstep to another. For you to travel anywhere without so much as a bow. Without fear of misdirection. The security guard at the door rattles prayer beads behind his back. Another counts tourists through the treasury chamber to a Minbar where Mary rings the dome, holds her immaculate son on the divan's white eiderdown. That you could walk from the Malfili of Murad aligning yourself with the blue/green mosaics and speak your name: Allah. Jesus. That the hand of another will carry you through the sky. The holy texts are bound by the same tiles but the Imam's translation of the ten commandments does not fit, says the guidebook. And yet all the gold in the bazaar passes beyond skin. On the diesis, a precursor asks Christ to intercede on the behalf of humanity. Hand poised, but the eyes look past you asking: why?

A blue dome's improbable fold leaves no room for error. How the light
breaks through. You do not trust it you say (since no-one can be trusted).
Don't tell them any names or dates. Wipe out the messages as you go.
A signature innocuous as the mark of a fingernail clawing at a wall.
No-one is working on Hagia's southern restoration, but the scaffold
remains. It has been like this for years now, says the guide shuffling in
a cast of expensively bored Russians. Place your hand in the column,
ask for someone else's luck. For the garden of Constance to unlock.
For the emperor's green door (güzel kapi, the Beautiful Door) to open
just for you. Dilek Taşi. Place your hand on the wish column. Sweat out
the mythamous of history. Laugh your tears aloud. Under Sofia, Medusa's
head is caught sideways by Perseus, Poseidon [insert other names here].
The column trickles down, 100ft filled, it's said, with the tears of slaves.
In the darkness you thought no one was looking, but he is here always,
changeable as sky: Christ to Apollonius. In the dark, unsure, unbeliever,
to pray beyond the everywhere corruptibility of it all. Because anyone
should be free to walk through a door and drink in this sun, this stiff air.

from **BREMEN → HAMBURG**

'PYRAMID FORM REPRESENTS HIERARCHIES'

To exist not to exist. To exist inside the betterment of a future.

Put your hands to your ears as in Munch's Das kind und der Tod. Say something back to the almond eyes of Modersohn-Becker's Mädchenkopf.

Beckmann's Sinnenda Frau turns and looks off into the grey distance. And still this throbbing.

An EU flag irises your hair. The Schipol falls into a rising sun. Hunter valley green.

To exist, inside the jaw of a caught whale.

World
spinning, don't slip
away.

Over Bürgermeister Bridge, children protest: one with a paper globe declaring KAPITALISMUS.

Child. Listen to the grown-up children who do not listen to you. They are wearing tailored suits and speak inside the static of world-wide radio. Android corporate on speakerphone. The sponsor for tonight wears a logo called JOKE. The replicants are laid out like stencilled furniture under heat lamps.

Child. Someone decided this is X. The exact point where the aliens will land.

Du spricht. Keine. Keins. The dayweight lump in your stomach.

You wait inside the absence of a window, count a sparrow's footprints. Malt of sleeplessness. The room cleans itself when you close the door.

Animal in a sensorial zodiac. The auditorium waits for you to speak but you cannot remember yourself beyond the functionaries of language. Two hundred hearts beat in mirror wind.

In heavy-breath silence, the culture secretary's jewellery titters. Everything gold down to the subtitles.

Because touch touches everything, moves through everything. And yet, nothing touches you.

As if life meant waiting for someone else. Don't touch me.

You write a letter to Gasquet on the riverbanks of the Weser. Nothing more than a creak in the wind of language.

You write: your tribunes are filled with silt. Strike it out. Revision: your tributes are filled with the filthiest of secrets.

To edit yourself out. Another kind of dying. Your hair crooked in the photobook.

You drag your Hippolytean iron foot. A simple valgus. Hunnishly indecent. In the archive footage, Bovary's eyes twitch like the wings of a butterfly.

Talus. Fenêtre. Optimal storage of the eye. The beating skin of the canal. Time's colour, soured only by time.

The children
demand nothing,
only a planet.

A portrait of rain weeps into fern shadows of the lake. Get up from your attic posing, shake loose the blinds.

In the Gak, Cézanne's artillery war against Impressionism. Chamomile and cow parsley in the pallet of Monet. Paint the bloodbody. The soulfall.

Between gradients of catastrophe and ignition, you blanch at posterity. Live for a speckle of sunlight on the sitter's throat.

Blanched out. The field shucked to a sinew of roots. The sniper's eye misses, in-blinks. Pull your skin over your face and then what?

The hand-me-down of public view. Headlights stare, X-raying your face. Blue diamond backdrop. A flag in outskirt mud.

Don't go knocking on doors here. They have invented a name for your namelessness. '[T]he murderous bad breath / of some dictator / no one wants to know anymore.'

Anymore than you. Sprötze's little pepper sack. Bodies wrapped like silkworms.

PAKO graffiti. Swastika keys. Arrivals met sternly at the gates.

As if hate
could rival
yourself.

The cab driver at Hamburg was an interpreter for the US army in Afghanistan. Last year they refused him entry. So his family are at home and he's pretending to be here with you, driving through the veins of the Elbe.

What echoes. What coheres. Look into the light, away from sacristy, salvation. Away from yourself to the Hanseatic city.

U-shaped burnholes outstare the Baum wall. New recruits in khaki tread planks at Landungbruken laughing at Captain San Diego, Willy Brandt. Cigarette smoke cauterises through yellowy teeth.

On pleated water you float. Defence: a pageant of confidence. Platzen for Cartier and pleasured grimaces of the Reeper(bahn).

What brought you here and through which door does your conscience leave?

Inside the hipster hotel they are selling quotes from Goethe on the lids of jam jars. Umbrellas to pay for the rain. 'Wo viel Licht ist, ist starker Schatten.' Where there's a lot of light, there's a stronger shadow.

You tap-tap the ankerstock, nothing but wind. You jigger a gaff sail, nothing but stitches in the wind's mouth.

You ask yourself: what splits the world more: ideas of men, or men of ideas? Action or religion? Christopher Columbus puddling his pesto on the plate or Pope Alexander praying to the god of war?

Lepanto. Alexandra. Hamburg. Liverpool. Your losses. Your token demons nailed to the mast. Your squadrons anchored. Your race-built Galleon Bull.

And every little
ship overboard
with silence.

You sign off the Brevisma with ideas of Ascension. The bloodcake of the world sliced open. Held to the lockchain of Sklaven Ketten (kettled slaves).

You sign off the offsetted death rates with rationales of human merchandise tallies and space allocation. Just like the unfairness of Fair Rosamond. Nothing *great* about the Great Elector.

Beyond imagination, the wielding of empire. Sink inside your own mouth for a mother of pearl medicament box.

Pox on your Bredenhof, your Pollox. Brackish your Rumfass. Tyrell stares through the cracked paint of his face. Deadliness of certitude.

After the firestorm. After the dreadnought. After the patron seas of sailors.

To see the harpooned bone of the ocean. His acidifying face abhorred by the sea.

'Nimm meine Hand, und ich führe Dich zu Dir zurück.' Take my hand and let me lead you back to yourself.

Track your footprints in snow at the Berlin Victory Monument. You have been up all night, watching Churchill's greasy finger blot the sky with fire. Boil the stars of Europe.

Groggy, you search for coffee only to find food menus. From your window, Hafen City's dredged propeller, unmoved.

You enter the Kunsthalle, extended as pro-tag. Faces of gaping blank holes stare through the human graph where the only distinguishable word is HOPEFUL.

14.40 over 560. You write it down but do not understand the equation.

It is about making choices: tick the NERVOUS box or the UNEASY box. As if choosing between statesmen and businessmen.

If someone could tell you why the card measures at 4x3 inches for seven days in February, it might all work out right.

On the map, blue is Israel. Syria red. Palestine missing. The manifesto declares protest as anti-ammunition. If red is 40%, how do you live without it?

Weaponries meaning stock prizes. NATO receipts.

'A game is their history, / unbloodied, older than ours, / They don't need historians, / henchmen…'

And so, splinter music. And so, a clock ticks above the bomb. Step this way says the businessman. I can stop you dead like a rattlesnake's eye.

You save the date. 24th June, 2045. When the financial singularity crashes. When the visor finally slips from your face. Or else this and with clearface heavies to tell you about it.

Gross capital cut-ups intended as much as stampbook fixities. How low might you go for half a kilo of speck? Car windows for 2hr limits. Mosques turning grey.

Every small consolation tradeable. Skeletons at the money counter. The bugs have their own voices and Goethe has been looking down on us, the unplucked chicken.

Your face shrinks into lines. A man who can grow numbers on his hands waits to count you at the weigh-in.

If you want to know why all this is happening ~~I don't want to know why this is happe~~ try speaking with the on-dead.

You pull away from the handshake and listen in. One ear busy with the voices you hear between radio stations.

You wheeze on a cane-backed chair, too tired to sit up or speak
out, your finger on the dial of the late night local shock jock.

To talk with you, eye to iris, as if through a veneer of smoke.
The glass on your mother's portrait breaks in your hand and her
blood (yours) is speaking blood.

All elegy, a held note –

father, wounded
by language, what song
can you sing?

from Of Breaking Glass (2022)

for Robin, 1973-2020

First thing you remember –

kicking in panels of glass
as mum and dad
warred
upstairs.

It was the day
he tried to strangle me.

It was the night
she came at me with a carving knife.

Brother, how to bury the sound of breaking glass?

[..]

If I could wash the blood from your feet.

The tears that
tear.

Take off your skin –
quartz into silicon

white globes surround

the consent of oxygen

Take off your skin –
blush of atomical redness

so much molecular pressure

to live inside a life

Take off your skin –

grief's abacus of rain

death's hand-me-downs

cold certainty of the slab

Take off your skin –

vanish in a reck of flesh

into the exploding stillness

this shattering of sound

6 am slowfire. Heat steps along the Pinnacles,
a glower of sand at Trona, the valley's theatre
of dust evaporating over Panamint Springs
until Wildrose, where the dash locks on 100º.
Drive into Stovepipe Dunes with a medicine
bag flailing around the throat. What turns itself
on the hearing wheel of vastness gone quiet?
Stagecoach cactus basket outside the museum.
Estrangement as reticence. Metabolic, not quite.
As if I could find you without touch, like an idea
out of reach, yet reached for. As if being here
means the gallant outdoorsman, not your typical
tourist overlooker. Audition for the part of grief's
chameleon. Cut. The light still rises over your
shoulder. As if being here meant it were enough
to bear this absence without the absence of air.

<Alphabet of Losses, Artist's Palette>

A for Alison. Her brother gone yet conversant after a decade (Amber)
B who lost her father. Anything but 'dying' or 'death'. It is 'his passing' (Lime)
C who couldn't hold his mother's hand in the ambulance (Umber)
D who hit a 40 miles per hour sign doing 80 (Adriatic)
E who tried CPR before the second seizure. 'But why did you have to die?' (Abalone)
F fractalized by death. Who lives again after burying the sun (Fire Brick)
G for Gaia, your uncle gone and your umbilicus in a locked drawer (Tiger)
H in Jedda, winding up the memory box of loss (Maroon)
I grieving you. All the places we never went and went but never leave (Violet)
J whose parents died on the same day, apart but knowing (Cornflower)
K your mother and father in Derby, via Amritsar. 'Sorry' is never enough (Coffee)
L whose father's face kaleidoscopes in a bottle of single malt (Lava)
M for Mum. The laguna of burying your own son (Rose)
N still walking the penumbra streets of Dublin (Dust Brown)
O for Olga echoing in hallway mirrors (Ivory)
P nightshifting the emergency ward, masked to the eyes (Canyon)
Q who renamed himself the devil's psychic. Who is empty yet purulent (Ecru)
R for Tony: 'there's nothing that compares with the death of a sibling'. And he knew. (Purple Satin)
S for you, Sidewinder. Hissing like a mine (Sapphire)
T for Toby, carving the wood of his mother's coffin (Chenna)
U in Amaranth Pink, singing 'Rebel, Rebel' through the kitchen.
V for Li Wenliang. The Wuhan Whistleblower (Bone)
W who staked everything on a blast of new cells (Dark Slate Grey)
X for K Za Win, who shielded children from a rain of bullets (Fulvous)
Y the Shoshoni, at the hands of the so-called pioneer (Red Ochre)
Z your encore, your platinum laughter. Steel teal in a palette of loss.

To think of you at your lowest point
in the lowest point of the Western
hemisphere. Badwater: metabolise this.
Walk through salt. Wallblood. Sandhour.
Brother: nobody can harm you anymore.
Miocenic insignia. Glass inside clavicles
of rock. Quartz breath of oxygen. Agora-
phobia, the limping brother, heal with salt.
Unsuffer a life. No more counting cracks
in pavement slabs. Goodbye. A sudden release
of pressure. The city's gridded constrictions.
Be good to yourself and something good will
happen said the celebrant. Cloudshadow
unthreads Thorndike, drifts over Mahogany
Mountain like a form of breath released.
You, the child, the petrified angel, the adult
who always wanted to leave. Leave.

<*Zabriskie Point* coda>

To ex/plode. To survive beyond fridges and flying chickens. Weight of mirrors. Of libraries. The screaming glass of television. Rename it distillation. Splintering of the cacti. Your eyes must have wanted to protect me across the lounge room. Perhaps I only remember the hideous carpet. The lightning terror of my pulse. Maybe I was looking away. Looking down at the miracle of my newborn hand. Detonate the not-know. Ex/plode glass back into sand. Plosive flints on the road home. Just let the bully's try and find you now. Shriek quieter than an under-radar. Unheard even when the drums fingle in. Sound shaken back into shock comets. Beyond cobblestones of voice. The intimacy of shoes. Taken off. Taken out. Graspable yet invisible. What it is to live with you as air. Simple as breathing or screaming in the asphyxiation of dust. Can you see me through the daily mask. Smiling at you like water brisked by wind. What remains is the red cloth of grief. Still. The important things are never washed clean. Language names some/thing. Try writing the word 'glass' with a stick of fire. Detonation unkeeping you for company.

Let the living wardrobe you carried on your back. Loosen into kindling. A sound of glass passes the eye like tears of laughter. The pantry beserks. On the way down I'll catch you. I'm sorry, so sorry. On the way out. I was miles off. As if one day it will be as easy as getting back into the car and simply driving away. No. Silence in the song keeps playing through. Hear it to live with it. To converse you dead. To be comfortable with the screech in my skin. Sunlight dims a valley's concave horizon. Makes it sound easy as watching clouds migrate somewhere new. Close the door. Open the door. Childhood blue sky. Everyday threats. Hear those voices now you'll have a reply. Ex/plosion. Fire into air. Light it up. Not dressing as a wound. You're in charge now. Nobody good enough to give you a start writes the last scene. Fire the dark. Burn the rafters. Every window breaks open and walks through you. There's a hammer in your foot. Why shouldn't things be different now. No more blood left to give. The presenter on the screen disappears into sand. Nobody scoping you out on the street. Nothing left of fear. The onion world will skin itself. Tears in the urn. What was broken that was once you. Transmutes. Quartz into silica. The sound of glass (un)shattering. In The End. It hurts and never goes away. With us, but not. With us. It is always you.

from Mythaca (2023)

Aurora

At what dawn? Aurora sunrise, Chondote sunset,
orchard fields torched by Dearborn for lakefront
mansions at Peachtown. An outskirt sign euphemises
The Mound, the lives unaccounted for in Washington's
idea of scorched earth. Untrail to burial grounds looted
or unrecorded, but trees counted up in the thousands.
America collectivised to stake claims on a pioneer tale
of loss, positioning itself too distantly in the museum –
spear tips, little else but the uncasually picked artefact.
Henhawk's voice plays over reparations of copyright.

This is what you pay for the price of tranquillity;
a gate opens the shore where it once slammed shut;
ruins of an electrical mill adjoin the inn's masonically
uniform welcome, VIPs stepping out in LL Bean
costumes. At the dock, slushing ledger of secrecy,
flags white as Doric columns snag winter sleet,
leaves confetti-blown along the yard perimeter.
Towards the reservation at Union Springs, a sign
reads the 'First House' was built by a white man.
No. Another house was there first. A whole nation.

Mythaca

Men, ravaging the region of Calydon,
sniffing out boar's blood, woodsmen
on errands for Artemis ~~on Green Street~~
with a homesteader's supremacism.

Oeneus makes promises; vine grape
to vintage. Demeter, the seed's secret,
a mill of golden harvest. Ambition
plucks the spear from Atalanta's teeth.

Men: infernos dreaming with eyes awake,
~~on Clinton Street~~ severing the rock gorge.
Corpses buried deep as fossils to be sent
back to the capital lawns of Washington.

Boy Odysseus plays Polutropos, bargains
with his father to tell him the truth about
Ithaca. The real story of arriving home,
when somewhere else is your home.

Ganedagǫ

Henhawk said his grandmother spoke the name for this place.
For years, I did not understand it what it meant.

The word has to be seen to be understood properly. Displaced,
he could not see it.

We took the names with us out there. Ganędagǫ:. Ithaca. In the hill.
In this fog-rolling lake.

There is no entry for this in the coloniser's dictionary.

Fog severed by the pricked ear of a sailboat on Stewart Park. A
joggers blotted shadow.

Ganędagǫ:. In and of the hill. A word that has waited to walk
through a door for over two hundred years. Misplaced by the
key of language.

Inside the ceremonial house. The motherland. What the
freshman calls 'Engineering'.

Place, a keyhole. Displacement, in missing key.

An entire village was torched right here under your feet. They
do not want you to find out the name.

If you walk to the tower, you walk over the dead slope.

Mythaca. Gayogohó:no?. Ganędagǫ:.

The ashlar doesn't fit because the bones are still missing.

from Emanations (2024)

for Niall McDevitt (1967-2022)

1

Who outstared Balor's giant eye in Connacht,
and lit the fire under Lugh in London, vatic
activist, walking the imagination of streets.

Whose megaphonic clarity blunts the scrapers
blocking out our sun like modern millstones,
who is rageously out *because life is outrageous.*

Top-buttoned at the gig with the absinthe bar,
here's a candle to light your way, another swig
from the glass to say thank you, sláinte, salud.

2

Family the wound: your mother across the Irish sea,
and you sent away like a wartime child. Exilic,
to outman the old man's jealousy, you sleep in the cave
of a palindrome says legend – Niall, who offered to kiss
a 'loathly lady' for the sovereignty of Ireland. The idea
of unification in your name, the one good scheme that
might yet come from Brexit. Childhood as hostage,
Torna, poet-druid, found you inside a hungry gorge
and raised you among sages. At Syracuse, I catch your
enemy, Eochaid, on the runway, his cancerous Pictish
arrow smothered in silks of undercloud. Tomorrow,
fretful but thankful, to see you again on Ladbroke
Grove, resting in your open casket. Eyes close for
peace. Emanations: the Great Humanity Divine.

3

In the Blake interview you made, planting roots before
Paradise, a biblical phrase broke me down: *numbered,*
numbered, weighed and divided. Julie, in who your love
was synergistic, aura-entire, dresses you in suit and
polka dot Baudelairian scarf before I arrive wondering
how to walk the unmappable city without you. Redraw
the map you'd say. Steal a drop from Chaucer's
parturial fountain, fish out Shakespeare from his river
digs; the inner chamber of a London carpark explored
excavationally, one of the city's holy sites you said:
Will lived here. Stretch hands as if to channel fumes
of history. *His bedroom is beside that yellow Porsche.*
Mindwalk back to the nearest Wetherspoons. Someone
over their glazed roast and gold bar ale asks you your
name. Niall, a torch flame raised against Romano
Britain, who fought the colonisers of Leun Deun
400 years after Jesus first exodused in the desert.
Niall, you reply, smiling to touch the strangers glass.

8

Up with the milk,
un-caffeinated, I
mistake squares ,
Parnell for Fitzwilliam –
the Irish Writer's Centre warps
into the Irish Racecourse Centre.

You're a plasma, not a plastic Paddy
you said, when we were here
in the ancestral city (was it a decade
or more?) Under the streetlamps
of O'Connell, I met your father,
Michael – a collection of Meehan
peeping out his corduroy pocket.

From boulevard-wide streets,
slick with afterain,
a seat of purple rock aubrieta –
solitude of a convent wall,
your mouth grinning in gaps
of rockface shale. Sunlight flickers
green to gold in the stain glass
windows of Earley Studios –
the little sisters of the Assumption
stand on the steps, satchels in hand
(where do they go if not ascending?).

The building has been restored –
KEAVANS WETHERSPOON HOTEL
proud in its signage. Here,
we'd sit for a pint and I'd
request another airing
of your Orwellian satire.

A toast to Keavan. To fill
the table of its empty glass,
a blackbird builds a nest
in my hair. For this glass,
I'd swim the confluence,
stand before our fathers
and wash them clean,
so they might, in turn,
sit in place again before
their mothers. Mrs. Byrne
you called mine, though
she changed name years ago.
Absence bereft of speeches.
Best friend, best man.

Tonight, at the Teachers Club,
star in the film, but playing
truant, you walk with us again
through Joyce's secret wedding,
and the curtain weeps.

Across the street, DEVITT'S bar,
CLOSED   Across the road,
JERUSALEM, your dinery, OPEN

Jump

into the safety-

net of angels

into the winged air.

from The Overmind (2024)

APPARITIONS

Enter the interlude, the shadowbox, the waltz.

Re-
verse your voice first, then wake up
plumping the pillow –

attunally sounded out like

crystal
cut
dust.

Cello funeraries. Burnt gristle on the hook.

Once, I saw your face inside a mirror,
looked back,
swallowed myself
in the glass.

Charcoal outhouse, rooms,
pyramids. Mells of history.

We never thought of being alone. It kept me
from overfeeding the boy under my skin.

Tomorrow, how will you know? I've had to wait
lifetimes. Tomorrow, the idea of it could change
my name into redemption, or break it into pieces.

Tomorrow as midnight and, by morning, wind-
sieved, sand into sun, a path to light the dunes.

Tomorrow, or else and unless the song leads me
waiting on a dark-windowed car to arrive, its tail
strewn with black ticker-tape. Tomorrow as breath

blown

out

(not yet).

How long left to wait? I've shaken hands
with myself so often I know the dry con
tours, the underbones. Dread in the arc
of a question mark. You don't hear
something back like that and live un-
changed. It's not like one note is blue
when the echo is red, or what can be held
down by someone's idea of organic logic.

Same old friend,
same old sky –

I listen for you to enter
the empty room
at night.

I turn up the music until it

stops.

THE OVERMIND

I was wearing a jellyfish over my head. I could barely see at all –
must have fallen down a basement aleph, bumping off the steps.

I imagine it was the same way I fell when my mother was pushed,
my foetus six months gestational inside her. The sting made my skin

feel like it was being flayed and when I opened my eyes I saw
the walls shudder, as if mid-quake. I asked the doctor, what is

the distance between curse and symptom and she wrote out
her reply on a prescription pad: *it's like trying to measure the smell*

of death. June, the air thick as tar, a sixty foot truck came rolling off
Shore Drive onto 67th, smashing the side of the cab. I saw it all

in slow motion, wearing my jellyfish cape again, a tunnel of pixelated
shrapnel, the taxi driver's airbag an exploding green mushroom.

Someone groans. *Who are you?* Face pressed against the glass, blood
on the dash. *Turn off the ignition, turn it off,* then doing it myself, but

unable to pull him out. I emerged from the sky-tilted passenger side,
as if opening the escape hatch on a submarine, and jumped down.

A fireman mummified my hands, and we stared at the battered cab,
the driver cut from the windscreen before shock-vomiting onto the verge.

Glowing red and white in the ambulance light, a young medic said:
you were lucky, most people don't crawl out of those. I wanted to call

my daughter, Gaia, realising I could still hold her in my arms, see her
grow. Thank you. It is October, I have returned the jellyfish to the sea.

You've been given another chance said the doctor (strange term for anyone
on the brink of divorce). To survive, I must decomplexify everything:

no cigarettes, no meat, no wine, no love (not yet). It's too early to say
how things are going. One day I might wake up and not feel the sting.

IMITARI

How does meaning get into the image? Where does it end? And if it ends, what is there beyond?
ROLAND BARTHES

1

What is the first thing you remember in this world?

Being washed in tepid water,
a tin can bath beside an open fire –

all the faces candled and watching
through the darkness.

2

The image mismatched, precarious from the start.

That I am merely an extension of yourself,
too blind to see me.

What have I asked of you?

It is too much. Too much.

To imitate. To portray. To represent
the image like a memory of doubt.

Missense of abandonment.

A mare bucks

in an empty

field.

3

My father's eyes, murky from the drugs (morphonic?).
In the photograph, he comes round slowly in the chair.

Is the image, asked Barthes, representation resurrected,
mythic and antipathetic to lived experience? I cannot see

beyond it. In Avoca, before the dementia set, a yellowing
photograph of a spruced-up cowshed, the family house

where my father jumped over hedges all the way home.
We carry the portrait, asking locals: 'do you know where

this is?' 'Over the hill', gestures a man, but when we arrive
it's looks like another empty field. My father takes a bottle

from the back of the car and, standing in the absence of his
house, gulps the sting of it down. 'It was here, somewhere'.

In Bray, over dinner, he tells me who he is for the first and
last time. 'My earliest memory is being placed me on the steps

of a large country house to ask for money for the auntie they
abused'. Cutlery scrapes at silence. 'It was around Christmas'.

The image of my father recomposes itself, stares out the window.
'I remember' he said, 'there was a light snow falling on the lamps'.

Coda

Imitari, resemblance of memory. I have been portrayed,
represented, as if this were the fair copy of a life.

The first thing I remember, I was sitting on the toilet,
and fell in, convinced I was to be flushed down the dark

mouth of the drain. I remember a hot pulse of lightning
thrashed inside my body, before the rescuing of hands.

But no, this is not the first thing I remember. There was
a sound first, or the scattering of a sound, like an image

trapped in a kaleidoscope before shaken loose. Sometimes
I hold it up to the sky, and the glass around my brother

breaks.

from **EVA AT CLIVEDEN**

Eva, in service at Cliveden. Chromatic, blue blood, the seed.

Your undersong in the drawing room gone quiet, your face

shocked at the grate, a hand upon your shoulder. Eva,

you were panning the embers, not downing the sheets.

And he made note of your aloneness, your ability to keep

close with silence. And he watched you like a beam for roadkill.

In tomorrow's newspapers, one of his daughters will marry the
prime minister.

Lineage-hewn, embassic. Who could touch a man like that?

As the ambassador said to the banquet hall: green is the colour
of fine lawns and arsenic.

On the way back home, you tripped over your shoes. Red blood.

Eva, there must be a hundred steps from the garden to the river.

The hand lied as witness: only the stallion bucked in the stable
all night.

Eva, was the wind not listening? The wind is always listening.

Insist she be discrete and then be rid of her, they said.

The family tree. The severed bough. The blackened root.

There's nothing more that is to be done or said about it, they said.

And if you knew the child's name, you never spoke it. Eva,

great-great grandmother, tell me, who did this?

* * *

First, a five shilling note, as if accidently floating in the coal bucket. Every room

a crime scene waiting to be chalked. Speculatrix eyes

of the Jessamay, who would raze you, quick as a flash of lightning.

Over the fire grate, imperiously impervious and tied with a gold sash. A single note.

Ten shillings, a dairy of milk, bread and pheasant and no more a week of mutton.

All you have to do is slip the money inside your apron mantelet.

Close the door behind you and be who they want you to be, as darkness.

* * *

What is ash, if not time spent? I will not sign the visitor's book.

What is the sun to make fire? Tell me the names she would not

speak.

Who cuts the caesura of voice? A bell rings above the stable.

Where do you live in silence? In the silence of filthy hands.

* * *

Said to the footman, where's the hammer?

Said the baker: I would hammer their heads together.

Said the cook to the porter, if not us, nobody will take her.

Said nobody and never the cook to her master.

* * *

A butterfly house flutters with traps.

Ten shilling notes hoisted like flags above the fireplace, but what is surrender?

Given over, then hidden, like secrecy in the attic.

If a man finds a damsel that is a virgin, which is not betrothed, and lay hold on her, and lie with her, and they be found....

No-one finds him on the inside, except you.

Ten shillings stuck to a gold vase, to diamond-encrusted chandeliers. Fives between the banister, in the dust you swept and swept.

The music room spotless, but for notes wrapped around a harp, ivory keys of the pianola.

All you have to do is slip the money inside your apron mantelet.

A dairy of milk, bread and pheasant and no more a week of mutton.

Close the door and walk on through the dark.

* * *

Child, born to a family who didn't read, you read
Jane Eyre at night by candle, or from a looking glass –
faces *specking the gloom,* footsteps outside your door.
(Father, is it you?). Scent of beer rot and sweat, sound
of rushing wings, the shock of a pulse beating your ears.
Can I come in and we'll finish our little story? Was it
something like this he said? Bessie echoes a decade.
If family turns you over, it's the poorhouse or *something*
bad might be permitted to come down the chimney and
fetch you away. You sit it out for hours in the red room,
keep quiet, whisper your prayers and everything will pass.
(Father, will this ever pass?). This him and him, this
constant taunt of money. Rochester severs the bookmark.
Something bad that happened is happening again. Tulip
tongues wag, as if willing a *moment's mutiny* to light
the morning pink, a low sunrise on the parterre,
where they watch you watching them from binoculars
from the Octagon Temple. Your hand brushes orangeries
of flame azaleas, knowing how every leaf would stir a tea
laced with poison. *Why could I never please?,* Jane asks
inside the glass. You who endured too much of other
people's pleasure, underline *Silence! This violence is…*
most repulsive (they are repulsive) and *Master! How is he*
my master? (nobody masters you). The word 'nobility',
a lie old as power itself, there's nothing honourable in it.
You had a job to do, this was all. Cleaning out the grates,
putting out fires, until flammable, a match ready to ignite.

***

Said to the rag n' bone man: enough nails for a coffin.

Said the ratcatcher: inside their coffins I'll find them.

Said the tosher to the mudlark, it was his dukedom.

Said nobody and nothing was ever asked of him.

***

I have a dream of setting fire to you and you go up in a great pile of money.

The fire kindles your sidewhiskers first, then your eyes, black to bubbling.

The foals from the stud come out
shrieking

but there's no sound
from their mouths.

And then the dream
snaps shut
like in the gap before
waking up where

what you did to me was more real than anyone could think in real life.

Anyone but me.

I wake daydreaming at the grates.

Twenty shillings

left by you
(if not you)

at the hearth.

Richest man in England oh noble savage oh

to clean your house afire.

* * *

My great-great grandmother Eva walks past the Grand Avenue larch trees for the last time. Water in the Fountain of Love, pawprinted mud, the duke's hounds chasing squirrels at dawn. Why is it the rose garden wilts dry, as if its petals had been pressed in a book? She does not care for the question, looks straight ahead at the manor, once a fortress. A bag of nails rattles in her apron – poltergeist among living ghosts – a hammer raised in her hand and the seed of a child to raise in her stomach. *Nobody will believe you,* he said, *and the bastard will work the grates just like you* he said (and, yes, little Nora, she did). Slip the hammer inside your pinafore, its head weight bearing against the umbilicus. Born of sin, of violation, you must let the child live. The story of a father, an unknown soldier in the Boer War. This is what you will tell her. They never found him, he never came back. You walk through the servants entrance for the last time and begin at the southern terrace, dark with dawn shadow, the whole house still sleeping. Light the candelabra, to see what has been left overnight and every day for the past week; an envelope in the fire grate stuffed with shillings. *You would do well to take this,* he had said. And by god, you have taken it. With one blow of the hammer, you nail the envelope to the wall. Money, its failed spell, dangles from the partition. Enter the drawing room, another envelope, another nail in the wall and the manor wakes up amazed, the duke in his Ceylon robes, bustles down the staircase, the dogs going off, but you hear nothing. In the library, memory retches, his hand on your dress, pulling you down and further. You nail the envelope to the desk and, when he opens the door, enraged but hesitant, you raise the hammer again above your shoulder and shout *Back. Stay back!* Confusion of eyes, the dilemma of power to protect itself above everything, he steps back. *You, foul sir, would do well to take this.* Dignified and calm, you stride out the terrace exit – thick fog, steps to the garden, to the river, where the Thames appears to rise with smoke.

AMERICANS TALKING ABOUT GUNS

Take away the gun, he said, and you
take away the history of this country.

The gun of this country pointed
at everyone – from neighbour

to State, at the head of my son. Inside
the gun of this country is another gun –

congress, filibuster, capital,
murder. The gun of this country

someone else's country – nations
who called it by other names: mothers

and gods. There's nothing more
relaxing than a morning on the range.

This AR15 shoots straight as a dime.
Every time. Hold it. The gun covered

with blood. I keep everything in this
rifle cabinet loaded. In case they come

at night. I pay attention. I know what's
out there. One day they're coming and

I'll be ready. This rifle is my temple.
It was my father's and his father's before,

and his too, down to the years it took
to *settle* this place. A bullet from that gun

ripped a hole clean through your British
flag. I pray to this gun. I talk to it, as if

talking to my ancestors and to you,
my protector. Father, son, holy spirit.

327 people shot every day in America.
Over a third shot and killed. Every day

23 children and teens, 6 dead. Every day.
As if you can't just act on the stats.

'My ten year old daughter could shoot a baby
deer' he said. 'Straight through the heart

from 30 yards. She's *that* good'. The figures
omit injuries caused by civil insurrection.

OF DESIRE

I have written about this. A desire to communicate,
to obfuscate. Desire: transitive verb. What I want /
long for / crave is in a state of constant change.

I told you what I wanted but forgot to mention every-
thing else. How, desirous, I do not know what I want
and may not want what I know. How, fluxive, sometimes
I am thinking about Nietzsche, sometimes I am thinking
about boiling a kettle. My body is chemically different
in the morning than it is in the afternoon. Fissured,
polyvocal, cameo, transindividual, occasioned, multifocal.
I, I. Selving, cast into the inevitable shattering of the sea.
Where did you go? I am here, over here. I can't find you,
turn away from the light. Sometimes I want to call you up.
I pick up the phone and tap out the numbers but hang up
before it dials through. What could we say to each other now?
All grown up and stretching out the limits of our childhood
skin. I didn't call. What with everything else we might say.
Desire to speak. To be given space: infinite requests
made against silence. I'm repeating myself. What might
yet nourish me is incomplete, intermittent, ever-shifting.

Let me start again…

I am left unfulfilled. Incapable of sustaining a fixed self,
therefore easily broken. Trying and failing to learn
the river's humility. Sometimes it's just the wind
making my eyes run, sometimes I walk in the woods
for a sure place to hide. These things may be seen to help,
but there is no cure. Desire, always residual with lust,
since language itself is erotic. I have written about this,
I have been saying these things for years. Whole days
lost inside my footsteps, trying to wake myself up
from myself. How to move in and out of stasis.
Simple acts of daily transformation. Perhaps I could

refine it better with hindsight, not overly pressurised
by the syllables inside my mouth. How I want to offend
my own basic literacy. I, a labourer's son carrying
plank rot and a bag of nails, a blundering detective
who cannot solve the clues to his own case. I demand
a fresh enquiry after the enquiry. I am unfulfilled.

Let me start again...

It's a kind of self-dentistry. I have written about this.
To be remade, or increasingly fractured. To recollect
the boy in the photograph. Always the crisis: to change
into something else. A tightening of skin around hard-
bitten nails. All I admit to is the writing of the writing.

[. . . . .]

My brother, living in the ellipsis, wrote the missing line.
In night whispers, in dreams, his body appears through
a blood-spotted sheet, a keyhole inside a golden dome,
where he announces himself as medicine. How am I
to take this? Desire unstopping, yet continuing to flow.
Brother, among banished mothers, diminished but yearning.
You were just a little boy who could not just reach out
and touch him. Shelves of Freud. Always the dead father.
I write to him, the wisher, the one whose desire was denied.
I've been thinking about this for years, but didn't speak up.
How what resurrects, refashions the dead. How I tried
to build a mosaic out of his absence. In the rest chapel,
I held his hand, blood-drained, and noticed how his eyes,
once so vivid, had sunken back into their skeleton. I
wanted to view him more starkly, as if more complete,
but turned away and wept onto the pages of scripture.
It only ends with us. Only in death is the end of desire.

ISOLATION

April foolery. A page torn from the morbidity report. Contact tracery over a new contract. Just kidding. In Fuller's idea of quarantine the pope merits paradise. Virus as in pus, emanation. Zip up your semi-permeable protein coat and wait on the terminology of what it means to be tested or super-spread against index reports. I am telling you all this in the strictest of non-confidence. See Miriam's phrasebook on contagion and communal living. Page 7: what you cannot see, the fomite exposures on your door. Addendum to footnote on page 14: Social distancing also meant where you could sit on Boston Common, on the Greyhound bus to Newark. And so on.

Outer body postured sideways. Distract yourself. A three hour hunch and suddenly a paper moon lights up the room. Stock market effluvium. Yeah, the business is going to get a sock to the face alright. Easier to implode on remote. Voice against the rescue gate, plot bakes. And so on and so much for the holes in someone else's breathing. As if the wind blew open your mouth this aghast. Or Attila at the lectern might realise coma's more serious than money. Remoted. Dark blood through the tube repeats the joke's on us. You call and call, but cannot wake up the deepsleep.

Cuídate amigo. Cuídate. But nothing comes back. Closer to home and the business bee of friendship buzzes over an oeuvre. Time now to dust down my plans he says. As if writing relied on sure foundations. Ta for all that *stuff.* The act of consumption, feather to bone. Striven like a horse troop, and where does it get you? Death nearer known, slapped too hard on the back for coughing. Cough it up. Force yourself to look away from the window. A spider circles its web, eats the cocooned wasp. Vanity, forgive us this loneliness. All these barriers to song. Before summer comes, the entire sky will be pockmarked with perspiration.

Carnally hygienic. Zigzag past dog walkers texting from the leash. Subdolent. Quiet. The kind wind has nothing to do with. Blades shucked with dew. Sniff of the living will against your muzzle. Beautiful world it was, hiding inside a mazework of tree bark. How to climb your branch, giving up for so long now? Get up. Take the plane with a doctor's note flailing from your left pocket. Tend to your mother's cracked femur. Rage, rage, as Dylan commanded his father. Addressee returned from letterman who has signed directions to an exit. Interstellar, light as darkness, not yet. First, we stand this field. Wheat yet to spike the grasses.

Attempts at communal singing, as if this were what language is. Stuffed bears at the window. Angel bear. An orangutan flanked by pink hippopotami. The consolation note's opening line does not write itself. How to bear up like samphire against the weight of a sea? Bunting's oaks grieve: *sad is spring to perpetuate*. Time's (un)matter. The tilled soil melts in your palm. A wood pigeon looks on, impervious. Two squirrels scuffle against a shelterless tree. Freeze-frame, a pose made just for us. What can you say to the she-grave veiling face after face after…? That there may not be a country for the dead. Through low sun, I hear your thieving cackles, Mr Magpie. Click of the starling, a faulty telephone wire signals the cut line, the family omen.

[April 5th, 2020]

PARADISE STREET

for Chris, Pascal and Sarah Ellen Byrne (aka 'Nellie')

A friend psychohistoricises
how sexually-transmitted
diseases once lived inside
a museum curated behind
this bus station, vanishing
at its sexual peak.

Walk through the lube
of invisible walls, past
syphilitic vitrines, exiting
the museum door onto
Paradise Street where
sailors clutched the gates
for ordinance, safe passage.

Above us, the unwritten city
records how the poet
Gerard Manley Hopkins
was unrooted by Liverpool,
stock-still outside the museum,
waiting for a bus to the future –
Hopkins, thin, young, a sexless
virgin in Jesuit robes, a genius
in the offing, yes, but
blasphemous to any Scouser;
to talk the city down
in your letters as 'museless',
what a useless cold lie
of a thing to say.

Hopkins: look in and out
of the water, the Pool's
reflection, nervewires vibrating
from the Mersey source. Perfect-
pitch you had, tuning-forks
for ears, unreceiving the city

that sang (three times) of love.
Across the street, Jung's dream
as direct transmission, Liverpool:
'that which makes to live',
activated at night, travelling
in its song, amusing to some, but
cloistered to the protomodernist /
Victorian, god-lost at the dock.

Hopkins, unmanned, unkind to Liverpool
as fourteen years of the Tories.
Your muse forgets to look
for itself here, lonely along the banks
at Waterloo, happier in suburbia –
Lydiate, Town Green, waiting
on doubt inside the station
waiting room, listening to winter
storms whistle under the door.
Your muse shipwrecked, adrift
from floating on the 'Pool of life',
unknowing what the city knows,
that we must change to survive.

Androgynine Celtic electrolight,
uncontainable by any hierarch.
The headlines read the same thing.
Tories out. Landslide majority.
Twilight reclaiming football-
quiet streets, an afterparty quick
as the turning of a road. Red walls
rebuilt, extra time won, the city
briefly changing its clothes –
costumes for the late night dress-up.
Concert Square curios walk the mile,
everyone but the bride wearing
black, cat burglars with names
on gold sashes made to look
like money, the bride smiles,
her mouth a ship lit with sun.
Geordie stags, Belfast hen-heels

clipping towards bouncered doors
on Mathew Street. History in the lines,
sleeping inside hyphens, those who were
born here and the others passing through.
A Liverpolitan, I pitch-pint in, the wish
to live communal as a union. Dinesh,
his utopic vision of a one-world city.
Liverpool, the first black community
in Europe, but the karaoke machine
jams on the chorus, docks formed
by slavery waves, proximal points,
hellships counted as human cargo.

Through the green gates of Paradise,
the muse evades her museum,
henchmen sing in a patchwork of masts,
a working chaos of goodbyes,
arrivals, fishing boats from Wales,
ice-frigates thawing from Norway,
ghost ships from the Caribbean,
gifts sent boxed up from London,
through a tapestry of nets.
With its hollyhock eye,
the distant lighthouse ushers in
a single ferry from Dublin –
chapters of a life vesselised,
yet to be written, but already
moving towards my unborn body
like smoke breathed in secret.

Sit still, she says. Straightens
the ends of an Irish silk dress,
and considers what to do, how
to climb from the rocking boat,
my grandmother, steadying up,
shushing her three children,
one underarm, my father –
blue eyes yet to turn on full heat.
Come along boys, an unknown
man helps her with everything
that would fit inside a wooden box.

How to slither along the gangplank
when the waves slosh about like this?
Assimilate, side-to-side with the life
you had along with this opening
of a new life? Kaeliodescopes turn
the absent image – her husband,
my grandfather, across the Irish sea.
He shuts off the radio, the Trouble,
to which he is already too close.
In his chair beside the fire, a pipe
heaped with ash, he waits on news.

In the quiet darkness, what
must he say to himself? It is
not enough to know of hard time.
His wife left to look for work,
sending back money, sometimes
letters. *It's tough, love, I'm working*
three jobs. We all await you. Love, N.

My father at Milton's cottage,
nappy-towelled, gurgling beneath
his mother cleaning shelf ladders,
a mystery of books (it was the job
she enjoyed the most, the house,
now a museum for Milton).
My father, a man old too soon
in his 70s, doddering with dementia,
toddler-like at best in the care home,
as he was back then, seeking Paradise,
regained, lost, regained, lost and so on,
learning what he will know one day
and every day now, how it is to forget,
snatching at fragments of a world.
Ancestral laundry in a high wind.

[....] [....] [....] [....] [....] [....] [....]

A hand at the landing gate,
beekeeper-delicate, holds on
to the box that holds everything.
On the train here, I rode backwards,
as my father does, but better able
to hold onto the story of a minute,
an hour flashing past, as if for him,
unable to unmanage himself.

The return train is late. Loop
round to Moorfields, listen in,
with my accent of southern,
nomadia, thankful to a decade called
home. Streets swell in the echochamber
of my grandmother, who landed here
and knew what to do, the Liverbird
her spirit animal and guardian –
a gold icon at the gates of paradise.
For this, and for her to die in peace,
she must save, service to service,
the fortunes of a broken family.

Grandmother, I never met you.
You arrived at Paradise Street,
too soon, too late, your last words,
written of my father: *Tell Patrick*
I love him. His dinner is in the oven.

[….] [….] [….] [….] [….] [….] [….]

We say goodnight after toasting
to those who left under archways,
tunnels, muses and museums.
Not so much a hug of farewell,
more like poetics, permission
to continue. My friends convince
themselves into a whisky nightcap,
an alchemically-induced bar –
that opens from a blank door.
Apprentice to mental travel,

the circuit rush of Bold Street,
the shadow-work of the Brow –
a cauldron of water swirls
off the dock and, from its rails,
I peer over the edge of history –
where someone held out a hand
to my grandmother and said:
please, can I help you ashore?

New & Unpublished Poems (2025)

THE SHADOWLINE

Between the kicks and the halfpence,
between the shadowline and the sea,
we were born in a wooden valley
of mothers and fathers so absent,
it was as if they had it in for us. We
left as soon as we could speak back,
for years knitting knapsacks from
handkerchiefs and straw. So when
the time came, we could just walk out
the door, leaving less the reprimand,
the tightness in an open hand. I said
I'd never go back, but I've returned
by the gale-end of the weathervane,
the valley's rye drying in my palms.

Brother, we had to leave here, faces
taxidermal at night, sweating eyes,
bearing their allegiances in public,
taxonomies of borders and clans.
If you drew a line at the memorial
garden, someone was always made
to feel unwelcome. You looked up
and saw the shadowline above –
possessive, blocking sun. Cover me,
you said, like an antimacassar, let's
wipe away the stain of our birth.
Thirty years on, I'm not sure we
ever did. Our family name still
floats over the bones of its grave.

DIS / GUISES

I am warm in my ice jacket, waiting for the deal
to be made. Reliant on ape impulsiveness, self-
reflex, and visible only in traces, nomadic steel,
everywhere yet concealed in the fading azure
of twilight. I was a scourer by trade, medicate
at the pillbox of the (im)patient, but ambition
(yours/mine) was stamped onto the ticket of my
birth, sparking flints, furling a red sail over Troy,
boulderizing Babylon. I must wear another face
in the morning. Chameleonic, friend-seeming. I act
decisively where you dither between the ants
and the strawberries. In churches, eavesdropping
on pew silence, slits between prayer and speech,
salting conviction with flakes of ash, a white flag
cored at its centre. I appear through every animus,
but my stakehold is the human animal, shrieking
at itself in mirrors. I should rival nobility by now,
but when you strip me back, I am merely a system
of secrecies rarely spoken and never close enough
to be caricatured or precisely imitated. I thrive
in the commercial flap, eyepatch over dreams,
so when you wake up it feels like double blindness.
I won't be the last graduate from The University
of Stoic Jokes. I fit money like a hugging dress,
choreograph hologrammic stage-kissing. I am
aeons, centuries, I cannot be outmonstered or
remedied with neckbolts. Look from the ship,
there I am, hotfooting over the icecaps like a ghost
of smoke. I feign a naïve air, offering no trigger
warning until the full shot is off. But, really I cannot
be blamed for anything, a conclusion you must have
got it all wrong, with your laws and taxes and endless
debate. How to pass unnoticed? You are so confused
even the cause remains unknown. I let the lapdogs
feast on the watchdogs, exit the final scene, side-door.
You might think I was deciding by the week, but
long ago I was made up, the bed pillow fluffed,

Baphomet's rose swinging from the thurible. I have
felt it from the beginning, ominousness to the idea
of time. They say I was born from the fires of Ghenna,
but I prefer the cold consistency of water, sea-grapevine
in the current. I manufacture crises, re-serve leftovers.
Anger fused with failure is my electricity, calamity my
wisdom. I should be placed higher, and when the bets
come in, I have already cashed the chips. There is
no evidence I really exist at all. And yet, my cage was
defiled, the bars bent back, the pit-chains broken.
For what is to come, I am as guilty as you are.

THE BANALITY OF POWER

Cargo units kept on file,
deleted under investigation
by order of the management.
A bawdy euphony after
so many decades, eras,
knowing how to fit in,
twizzling my bow-tie
among the cruel gentry,
leasing budgets via chart
logic, weekly targets
for Christmas bonuses.
It's nothing personal, just
business, if you are wearing
a face, I can't see it. Vertigo
ascendent, the winnings
come in too fast to tally
(though counting is preferred
to actual conversation).

I don't want to know
your name, it's why we
assigned you a number,
as bankers and jailors do.
This is how I speak to you –
one hand over my mouth,
the other fleecing your pocket,
a kind of missive, plosive
in the middle of a global
heist. Makers come and go,
I've made mine already,
paid in full, by you, thanks
I might say if it weren't
like offering poker-play
consolations to the loser.
I work on you as pleasure,
trophic, the smell of a fresh
hide nailed to the wall.

THIS IS AN EMERGENCY

The climate emergency is our third world war.
Our lives and civilization as we know it are at stake.
EXTINCTION REBELLION

Operator: we cannot keep making the call.
Connect me so I can get through to someone.
Last time, a conversation, barely, a redneck
who, every summer, turns on all the lights
in the house, full blast, the gas and the oven,
standing in his garden with the hose on,
laughing at the sun. He believes his guru
of chaos that it's all made up and couldn't
understand a word I said until the line went
dead. Operator: a call to civilisation, that we
might listen to species alert, coral degradation,
the egg unincubated from the sea turtle,
the golden toad already gone – not enough
water to hydrate or reproduce as propellers
turn for private flights across the Cape.
This is an emergency, a last call, a war
charged against the power of all nations
(but is beyond nation). The life of life.
It is too precious to be put on hold.

A FLUTE FOR BOUDICCA

Don't forget we are dealing with barbarians
TACITUS

To the ancient Britons, the Romans had not only abused their queen and her daughters, with Boudicca being their earthly representative, priestess or perhaps even the embodiment of the goddess, Andraste, they had desecrated the gods as well.
VANESSA COLLINGRIDGE

When language leaves, all you
have left with is tone, all you have left are
smoke signals. I didn't know she was
using her own body as wood.
VICTORIA CHANG

What to take, what to leave behind?
Breath in a blackened flute shaped
like a heart. What the low notes refuse.
Dust and sediment clog the tone holes.
Seed-arid, everything that grows tested
in soil, liquid shadow, proof in the blood
but, somehow, remaining disfigured.
What the eye mistakes for lack of notice.
Hauntable objects formally elusive, scent
trapped inside a keyhole. Galleys sail
ocean strangeness, widening into fleets.
Criss-cross, out of form, like tea leaves
unread. The future myriadic, seen in
glimpses, hiving off the eavesdrop,
listening out-in-out-innate, stunned
into speaking, voice unskeletoned.
Upturn the bowl, a face locked outside
the awkwardness of being considered
infinite as personality, but unknown
so deeply each image appears more intimate
than a last look. Jagged across the page,
inveighed by Roman hoopla. Performed
as entertainment, calligraphic between
knucklebones, jokes about recklessness –
a woman astride her chariot, sage-smeared.
Note the furnace-blown sense of injustice

gone quiet. Words signalled back into
smoke. Reopening the medicine bag –
rose quartz, onyx, bitter pearl, black
tourmaline. Smudged on arms. If you
are who you say you are, I must be
careful among roots of heather, knowing
above the symbol and its trickster. How
love spars with death to enhance itself.
I turn over the cup. It is not the same face.

Scry helical. Double mirror. Scry
backwards, further than history.
As Tacitus said: 'whoever were
the first inhabitants of Britain,
whether natives or immigrants,
has never been answered: don't forget'
(the echo deadly across centuries)
'…we are dealing with barbarians.'
And how might you *deal* with them?
The druids of Mona knew power,
summoning fog from the elements,
beyond godly ideas of how we might
wear surfaces of character. Triads suggest
the blessèd whilst cleaning stained glass,
hierarchical with ideas of dignification.
Through field smoke, written in with such
certainty. But any queen complexifies
beyond name, victory or loss. Brute force
main-sailing Victoria's sea of empire.
That Rome would do to her and her children
what should never be thought, less done.
Flogged beside her daughters who were then
raped in front of her. This is how the eyes turn
into fire. Passing hands that petrify flesh.
Scry forwards. Maiden sage, motherwort,
anything to light up the stripling wood.

Where the dragons live, Cartimandua sits
within an army of roots, drawn by others
as though the breath of angels. Here you
found me hissing inside my own shade
like a tree that burns but will not burnish.
Remembered living in blazes, peacock-
yowling inside the cold cairn, a face
curlicued as the eyeholes on old trees.
Soul chambers in a mandala of feathers,
unseasonable leaf fall encradled with
crystal-franked incense. Grief chants
of neighbours. The Trinovantes enraged,
torn aslant from their oak path home.
Cries inside a cud hut. A rutted lane
made by hands weary of bending
back bracken and hedgerow mist.
Cartives seeking hyenas in petticoats.
When it's said but unrecorded, someone
always douses the facts, enough to spout
the origins of fake news: that fire might
be whetted down in public. Claudius
reshapes Tacitus, who first embellished
Caesar's diaries. Welcome to Rome.
Here's a ticket to the circus. If these
trees could speak, you say, I wonder
what they would tell us of ourselves.

Seneca, in his Apocolo, wrote of how he
'ordered the Britons beyond the limits
of the known sea. And the Brigantes
blue with their shields, to surrender
their necks to Roman chains'. Back-
stabbed at the senate, but the thirst for
murder lives on. Briton, shore-shingled,
fearing tidal waves of morning blood
lapping in through grimoire fires. They
who have slain Zeus for Jupiter, scroll
tight maps (ignore the tongue flapping at
Caistor). Claudius, who must appease Drusus
and his god, sees flames in the eyes of Caratacus,

but unsees, her, metted out for justice. What
more is this but the ill will of a collusive king?
Hide like trees, she said, as seers watchful
to evade the enemy's spyglass. Ask village
to homestead, the raising of family arms:
if we don't stand up next it's our heads
on the sticks. Photosynthesis in reverse,
fallen branches, ivy trails snake the gate.
'By me thou shalt cast out wicked spirits.
By me thou shalt know the doings and practices
of evil men and more than may be spoken.'
Fire from air. Unlooking for variants:
Roman, slave, enemy, Briton. Unburied,
tortured. There are other names for this.
The bones that sleep still missing a queen,
to whom you do not wage or bow, but
run with, together, across captive soil.

Scolded to light the flame. What
Tacitus and Dio fail to tell. Night-
spells cast against tithe-bound invasion.
Two thousand years plus of capitalist
clues in the senate fighting back blood
from the sword. Landlocked at cliffs.
Tacitus forgets standing on Tarpeian
Rock. Dio, the pickling jars, beheads
marking borders, spikes at Colchester.
Footsteps looking for exits, a spare cart,
a steady rowboat over the Thames
of Londinium, sacked, its real estate
prosperers sizing up St. Paul's before
patronage saints it. Underground run
the tunnels of Christ but, before he lived,
a temple, the largest in tribal Europe.
Enemy clans about-turn into friends
for a cause. To bury the undead and
avenge Rome. Enter Verulamium from
the scut road. Paulinus frets over Nero's
rages, waits before inflating the figures:
70,000 dead, and the harvest gone to seed.

She loosens a totem hare to run the line
of attack. Woods at the rear meaning no
ambush. Calvary troops nestle the slopes,
hopelessly, it seems, outnumbered. Paulinus
surveys the field – *gladii* come close enough
to twist into blood. 'Better to have poverty
with freedom than wealth with servitude'
moralises Dio, not believing it for a moment,
ventriloquizing until the deep fake is all
that is left. Sheer recklessness in losing
to anyone, but a woman? he questions.
Barbary to the breaking of cups at the senate.
Mancetter. Primrose. Towcester. Shadow-sided
Chiltern Hills of childhood. *Gladius* illumined,
shining on skirmishes sharp as a secret,
protecting house and rank. Paulinus meets
Boudicca. Far from the hills of Aventine,
flanked by her progeny. This is why we war.
No talk of retreat, nothing of surrender.
But the hare darts right, meaning wrong.

Emerald-eyed over Verulamium,
scanning scenes before they happen,
the layman's definition of strategy.
Nero tunes up his lyre, reverses coins
to appease Apollo laurelled, handing
keys to Artemis, god of the hunt
unrelenting, until it finds you out,
who knows where, but pressed
beneath the space of an emperor's foot.
Briton burning beneath the screed
of the tesserae, ash to be swept from
stokeholes, grave-shallowed, barely
traceable except by detection, luck,
or sheer instinct. On later coins,
the inscription reads VICTORIA AVGG.
Duplicate heads of state, decrying
Victory. East meets West, slave-carried
by conscript. Roman grapes, taken
from everywhere, sweet as blood.

Before called Devil's Dyke, before
such *daemons* existed, the tread of
a foot unwelcome. Fomoire's, once allies,
until the monster swims ashore. Blackbirds
tuft nests, remind of safe distance, the threat
of Latinate crests; Caesar's men still learning
names for the Second Coming, slithy off
the coast, scything back wheat, Gaul-haunted,
blades wet with entrails. After so much war,
the taste for it honours no-one, but the emperor,
stuffing scabbard knives into the pockets
of his generals, to arrive here. Round the back
of a pebble-dashed council estate. Places
where the poor continue to be kept down.
Where Cassivellaunus lays cloak and arms,
bowing to his new lord like a wounded vassal.

What Dio and Tacitus never felt,
nor saw in the invention of maps –
held breath beneath beech trees
at Watling. Far from wooded cairns,
what is called home already burning.
Innocence violated, sister warriors
who cannot share the same memory.
The hare is laid down, sniffing tricks,
it turns, sensing ambush, darting
in the mind, to change course, and so,
the course of the known world. A copse
hushed by Paulinus' hand, delayed,
waiting for the sun to hit his spear.
'Barritus' murmurs to a roar. A spectacle
fit for any colosseum. Run sisters, for life
that you might survive this. Andraste,
drinking down your mother's breath.

Immanuentitumnus of this earth, not excelsis.
Lost in fields of imagination or lip-synched
by the Romans. I offer this blackened flute,

luck's ruin unmade, for you not here,
but everywhere in the idea of England.
Knotwork branches cut for clearings, voices
in wind patter before rain and its silence,
enough to stiff the lips of men awaiting
golden coins. Fix the bronze triskele
around your throat – curvilineals unfold
into fire, ash, air. Laima, Mãra, Andraste,
Boudicca, free your daughters, enfolded
with spirit imbued. I walk Caesar's Road,
Conquest Hill, carrying the bones,
shaking dust from boots, pine needles
stuck to my foot. I scatter rose petals
on hawthorn branches, and watch
a hare bolt keenly through the field.

AT THE VALE GATE

Father, happy new year,
slippery as air, our first
without you. We service
loss into an idea of order,
dates, celebrants, timings,
people to invite, and not,
try for a way that is soft,
soft, to trace the dust
and expel winter's flaw.

Father, at the vale, I wait,
an impatient guest, remiss
to the task of losing you
again. Branches severed
from the morning storm,
a wind-spindled sky,
blanket grey in uniform.
Soon, the threat in a word,
the euphemisms, cards,
kindly reminders, yes,
I'm sorry for your loss.

*

We die years, lifetimes.
The body at rest, the spirit
thirsting to make space.
In a daydream, you wake,
washed clean of skin,
smiling as you leave
the cottage, the old shed
made good, built by hands
that held you in life. Father,
it is time for you to go.
Close the gate. Light
untangles from hedgerow.

I kiss your brow, fold
your clothes inside a tree.
I fill your glass with love,
and drink sweet its shadow.

NOTES AND ACKNOWLEDGEMENTS

The poems in *Nightsongs for Gaia* were first published in the following collections: *Passages of Time* (Flipped Eye, 2003), *Blood / Sugar* (Arc Publications, 2009), *White Coins* (Arc, 2015), *Everything Broken Up Dances* (Tupelo Press, USA, 2015), *Withdrawals* (Knives, Forks and Spoons Press, 2019), *The Caprices* (Arc, 2019), *Places You Leave* (Arc, 2022), *Of Breaking Glass* (Broken Sleep Books, 2022) and *The Overmind* (Broken Sleep, 2024). The author would like to thank these publishers and editors respectively. Brief notes on individual poems are as follows:

Blood / Sugar

'Apprentice Work' (p. 16) references the work of Peter Redgrove. 'The Gale Chambers of the Vast Nose' is a title from his posthumous poetry collection *A Speaker for the Silver Goddess* (2006).

'Air Terminals' (p. 19) quotes Katherine Mansfield's short story 'A Cup of Tea';

'Days of 1973' (p. 21): 'The kettle yearns for the mountain / The soap for the sea' is from Derek Mahon's poem 'Nostalgia';

'Sestina for R' (p. 26): the repeated and part-repeated lines in the poem ('Like a vessel too thin for certain vibrations') are from Edna St. Vincent Millay's poem sequence 'Ragged Island' (1954);

The Brain (p. 26) was a rave club in Wardour Street, Soho, London.

White Coins

'Economies of the Living' (p. 34) was influenced by *An Introduction to the English Reader* (1830), particularly sections titled 'Didactic Pieces';

Lu San (p. 38) is a Myanmar poet.

Everything Broken Up Dances

'Mallajah' (p. 46) was written after attending the Al-Sendian festival in Syria.

'Wild Desert Thyme' (p. 42) was written after participating in the Tripoli International Poetry Festival in Libya.

Withdrawals

'Silence, say something' (p. 60) and 'Left brain…' (p. 60) were written as commissions for the Bavarian State Ballet in Munich, Germany. The author was commenting on the work 'Borderlands', by dance choreographer Wayne McGregor.

The Caprices:

A book-length ekphrastic response to Francisco Goya's 'Los Caprichos' (1799). The Los Caprichos images which accompany these poems are part of the original 'Prado' manuscript, published by Dover Publications in 1969.

'The sleep of reason produces monsters' (p. 62) includes an echo of John Milton's 'On the Morning of Christ's Nativity' ("A Wakeful

Trump of Doom Must Thunder the Valley Deep") published in *Poems of Mr. John Milton* (1645).

Places You Leave
'Cox's Bazar' quotes from poems by Ro Mehrooz and Zaki Ovais included in *I am a Rohingya* (Arc, 2019). Other quotes are anonymised. 'Ze zaga añra félai ay zaígoí' (p. 68) translates from Rohingya as 'places we never leave'.
'Istanbul — Gaziantep' (p. 70): the excerpt from this text is dedicated to a Rohingya poet denied the chance of education in Turkey despite having a scholarship to study there.
'Bremen — Hamburg' (p. 72): all quotes are from *A History of Clouds* by Hans Magnus Enzensberger, translated by Martin Chalmers and Esther Kinsky (Seagull Books, 2018). Further quotes are from Goethe's play *Götz von Berlichingen*, Act I (1773) and from Ingeborg Bachmann's 'No Delicacies', both translated by the author. The collage on p. 72, entitled 'Pyramid form represents hierarchies', is by the author.

Of Breaking Glass
This sequence of poems was written in Death Valley, California, after the unexpected passing of the author's brother, Robin. The photograph (p. 84) is the author's, one of several taken in the desert and included in the original publication.

Mythaca & *Emanations* were published as limited edition copies in 2023 and 2024 respectively, and can be found in the Poetry Library in London. *Emanations* is dedicated to the poet Niall McDevitt (1967-2022). McDevitt was a London-Irish poet, musician, 'walking artist' and actor. The poem contains some excerpts from conversations between McDevitt and the author. *Mythaca* is also dedicated to the Gayogohó:no? community, with particular gratitude to the work of Stephen Henhawk and Kurt Jordan.

The Overmind
'Apparitions' (p. 93): the italicised section is from a track by Northwest entitled 'Same Old Sky' on their self-titled, debut album (2017). The poem is an automative, psychoacoustic response to the whole album. *The Overmind* is indebted to various poetics and poetic thought, not least Sri Aurobindo's philosophy and H. D.'s ideas expressed in 'Notes on Thought and Vision', republished in *Visions and Ecstasies: Selected Essays* (2019). The title poem mentions an 'aelph', inspired by the end of Jorge Luis Borges' short story 'The Aelph'.
'Imitari' (p. 96): the quote from Roland Barthes comes from an essay called 'Rhetoric of the Image' (1977).
'Eva at Cliveden' (p. 99) includes quotes from Deuteronomy and from the opening of *Jane Eyre*. The original grounds of the Manor are now

an exclusive hotel and National Trust site.
'Of Desire' (p. 107): parts of this text have been collaged and extended from a poetics written for the author's PhD, 'A Poetics of Desire' (2019).
'Isolation' (p. 109) includes a line from Basil Bunting, 'sad is spring to perpetuate' ('Briggflatts').
'Paradise Street' (p. 111) was written after an evening in Liverpool with Chris McCabe and Pascal O'Loughlin. It makes mention of William Blake's use of the term 'mental traveller' and Iain Sinclair's 'Liverpolitan'. Levi Tafari and Dinesh Allirajah are also mentioned. The early part of the poem is a critque of Gerard Manley Hopkins who said that 'Liverpool is of all places the most museless'. This poem is written for the author's grandmother Sarah Byrne (aka 'Nellie'), imagining her voyage from Ireland, carrying three children (including the author's father) and all their possessions in a wooden box.

New & Unpublished poems are from a new collection *The Banality of Power*, anticipated to be published by Broken Sleep Books in 2026. The sole exception is 'At the Vale Gate' (p. 129), written after the death of the author's father, part of an elegiac sequence called 'Sonships'. The early part of this poem bears reference to Shakespeare's *Hamlet*.

The author would like to thank various writers, editors, publishers and organisations who have supported his work over the years. These include: Arc Publications, Tupelo Press, KFS, Broken Sleep Books, Tony Ward, Angela Jarman, Aaron Kent, John Kinsella, Nii Parkes, Antony Rowland, Rosie Levine, David Spittle, Kirsten Norrie, Sandeep Parmar, Cornell, New York and Edge Hill universities, Niall McDevitt, Ilya Kaminsky, Forrest Gander, Valzhyna Mort, Ishion Hutchinson, Katherine M. Hedeen, Víctor Rodríguez Núñez, Paul Stubbs, Golan Hagi, Fred D'Aguiar, Sarah Crewe, Robert Sheppard, Alison Trower, Ro Mehrooz, Pacifist Farooq, S J Fowler, Alvin Pang and Chris McCabe.

BIOGRAPHICAL NOTE

James Byrne was born in 1977 near London. He has published seven full collections of poetry, including *The Overmind* (Broken Sleep Books, 2024), *Places you Leave* (Arc Publications, 2022), *Of Breaking Glass* (BSB, 2022) and *The Caprices,* a response to Francisco Goya's 'Los Caprichos' (Arc, 2019). *Nightsongs for Gaia* includes works previously unpublished in the UK, such as *Everything Broken Up Dances* (Tupelo, 2015) and the limited edition pamphlets, *Mythaca* (2023) and *Emanations* (2024).

As well as being a poet, Byrne is an experienced editor and translator. He edited *The Wolf,* an influential, internationally-minded literary magazine between 2002 and 2017 and, in 2012, he co-translated and co-edited *Bones Will Crow,* the first anthology of contemporary Burmese poetry to be published in English (Arc, 2012). He has co-edited a number of anthologies, including *I Am a Rohingya,* the first book of Rohingya refugee poems in English, *Atlantic Drift: An Anthology of Poetry and Poetics* (Edge Hill University Press / Arc, 2017) and *Voice Recognition: 21 Poets for the 21st Century* (Bloodaxe, 2009).

Byrne co-translated Libyan poet Ashur Etwebi's *Five Scenes from a Failed Revolution* (Arc, 2022), from which a poem was selected for the Deep Vellum anthology *Best Literary Translations* in 2024. *I Am a Rohingya* was part of the supplementary evidence presented to Aung San Su Kyi when she was invited to The Hague to answer crimes of genocide against the Rohingya people. Recently, for Arc, he co-translated, with the author Ro Mehrooz, *Poems Written Through Barbed-Wire Fences.*

At present, he is working on a collection of essays, and finalising a new collection of poems. Recent awards include a Cholmondeley Award and a Travelling Scholarship from the Society of Authors.

www.ingramcontent.com/pod-product-compliance
Ingram Content Group UK Ltd.
Pitfield, Milton Keynes, MK11 3LW, UK
UKHW040831050725
460397UK00004B/102